Praise for Chantel Lysette's
Azrael Loves Chocolate, Michael's a Jock

"In this inspirational, uplifting, and empowering book, Chantel writes not from shallow research or speculation, but from courageous, tireless, shamanic inquiry. Through her dazzling clairvoyant abilities, she is able to give us first-hand accounts of Divine archetypes some people have never heard of, much less conversed with directly. Chantel insists that if she can do it, you can do it, too, and in giving your 'magical' power back to yourself, she offers a way for you to have a personal relationship with 'unseen' angels and develop your spiritual eyes so you can peer into the gates of heaven."

—Amelia Kinkade, author of *Straight From the Horse's Mouth* and *The Language of Miracles*

"When it comes to Angels … Chantel Lysette is right on. What a wonderful book, getting to know angels on a personal level."

—George R. Noory, host of the top late-night radio show *Coast to Coast AM*

THE
ANGEL
CODE

© Britt Photographic

About the Author

Chantel Lysette is the creator and host of the highly acclaimed lecture/ reading series The Angel Gallery™ and the author of *Azrael Loves Chocolate, Michael's a Jock*. She is also a double-certified Master of Usui Reiki (a form of intuitive energy healing) and has over a decade of instructional experience in meditative studies, intuitive studies, comparative world religion, and philosophical studies. She lives in Southeast Michigan.

THE
ANGEL
CODE

Your Interactive Guide
to Angelic Communication

CHANTEL LYSETTE

Llewellyn Publications
Woodbury, Minnesota

First Edition
First Printing, 2010

Cover design by Adrienne W. Zimiga
Cover angel image © iStockphoto.com/Michael Knight

Llewellyn is a registered trademark of Llewellyn Worldwide Ltd.

Library of Congress Cataloging-in-Publication Data
Lysette, Chantel.
  The angel code : your interactive guide to angelic communication / Chantel Lysette.—1st ed.
     p. cm.
  Includes bibliographical references (p.   ) and index.
  ISBN 978-0-7387-2123-1
  1. Angels—Miscellanea. I. Title.
  BF1999.L97 2010
  202'.15—dc22
                                        2010012814

Llewellyn Publications
A Division of Llewellyn Worldwide Ltd.
2143 Wooddale Drive
Woodbury, MN 55125-2989
www.llewellyn.com

Printed in the United States of America

Then was brought unto [Jesus] one possessed with a devil, blind, and dumb: and he healed him, insomuch that the blind and dumb both spake and saw. And all the people were amazed, and said, Is not this the son of David? But when the Pharisees heard it, they said, This fellow doth not cast out devils, but by Beelzebub the prince of the devils. And Jesus knew their thoughts, and said unto them, Every kingdom divided against itself is brought to desolation; and every city or house divided against itself shall not stand: And if Satan cast out Satan, he is divided against himself; how shall then his kingdom stand? And if I by Beelzebub cast out devils, by whom do your children cast them out? Therefore they shall be your judges. But if I cast out devils by the Spirit of God, then the kingdom of God is come unto you.

MATTHEW 12: 22–28

Contents

EXERCISES

PREFACE

As I sit here looking out the window of my tiny bedroom down onto the busy freeway, I lean back in my chair, sigh, and wonder what in the world God has planned for all of us—for this reality we live in. In a life wrought with uncertainty, tensions are high, fears are soaring, and it seems as if existence itself is out to make a mockery of the beliefs and ideals we all hold dear.

Despite feeling that the world is spinning out of control, I still cling to the understanding that all this is God's Plan—from the rising and setting of the sun right down to whether Meagan across the street will land her first job with the local coffee shop this summer. But knowing that God is in control of what we may otherwise see as pure chaos doesn't help me with the feelings of dissatisfaction, sadness, or confusion that we all seem to constantly face.

There are times when emotions get the best of me and I scream heavenward, clutching my hair in frustration, "God, what are you up to now?" It is then that Archangel Michael appears, bringing his golden rays of sunlight with him.

"You chose this, Chantel," the angel whispers. "You knew, well before you came here, the world you would have to endure."

Well, that bit of insight does little to ease my discontent about the never-ending struggle with itself that humanity seems to be locked into. But at the end of the day, Michael is right. We all knew the turmoil we'd have to suffer when we chose to partake in this reality. It's as Archangel Uriel told me a long time ago—no one is here because they were forced to be.

We're all here because we want to be.

Given that, I guess there's little excuse to bemoan our dispositions and circumstances, our decisions and their consequences. We all came here because we knew we could withstand everything this reality had to throw at us. And we're here only because God trusted that we could handle it. Nevertheless, we are human, and subject to human emotions and frailties. This can create stumbling blocks along the arduous road of life we travel as we try to make our way back home.

I mean, that's where we're really headed, after all. Home to the realm of spirit, to the bosom of God (however you view him … her … it). A friend of mine once mused, "It's like God drove me out to the forest and dropped me off, spun me around, and left me with a compass and a Swiss Army knife to find my way back to him, some light-years away." The more I thought about this, the more I began to share that sentiment. I'm guessing that a lot of you reading this feel the same way.

I'm not saying God abandoned us. Not in the least. He's hovering quietly, watching to see how we do on this survival challenge. So we tread along like little children, trying so hard to be brave because we told Daddy we were big enough now to go it alone. But deep down inside, we're scared to death of the slightest shift of the wind and every little rustle of the leaves. We want so badly to call out and say, "I changed my mind!" But we can't. Dad told us, when he plunked us down here, that once he did that, there was no turning back.

And so the journey begins.

So here you are, trekking along a very set and directed path home (though you've no map that tells you this). Just because God isn't visible to our human eyes doesn't mean that he isn't present. Not only is he observing your journey, but he's sent your big brothers and sisters—the angels—to watch over and help you. It may seem like you're walking alone, but there will come a moment when you spot, out the corner of your eye, your brother's smile or a wisp of your sister's hair. You may hear your sister's giggle on the wind, or wake up after a lonely night to find that someone covered you with a warm blanket. So, regardless of obstacles or fears, you keep pressing along. When you reach the edge of the forest, you realize that you were never in any real danger—after all, you were only exploring your own back yard! And there on the patio sits Dad with a knowing grin. You run toward him with a beaming smile.

"I did it! I did it!" You jump into his strong, loving arms and hop up on his knee to tell him all about your adventure. You boast about how you fended off a big grizzly bear with a couple of pine cones. (In actuality, that was your brother Michael in last year's Halloween costume, but he did such a great acting job that you darn near wet your pants—although Dad doesn't need to know that part.) You tell him about how the fairies left you cookies and milk along the trail (when it was actually your sister Iophiel the entire time). You tell him about how the moon and stars were so bright that you really weren't *that* scared (and all the time, it was actually your father switching on the Christmas lights he and your brother Metatron had strung along the path to light your way).

Although you struggled with your fears and maybe even wept a little in the night, you were never really alone. Not once. You may have felt lost and as if you were going in circles, but there was only one path for you to take home—and your sisters and brothers were there to make sure you stayed the course. They planted clues along the road home...whispered guidance to you in your sleep...put up barriers blocking off where you weren't supposed to go...and cleared away the brush from the path you were supposed to travel.

It's all in a day's work for the archangels—keeping us humans, their spiritual siblings, aligned with God's Plan.

Regardless, walking the long, arduous road is no picnic. I think many of us can attest to that. But God wouldn't have us wandering this world languishing, nor would he have us wandering this world clueless. Time and time again, he sends his messengers to deliver words of wisdom and signs of Divinity's presence among us. But we're so caught up in our human drama—so distracted by what's going on around us—that we often miss these messages and signs.

It doesn't always have to be this way, however. The moment we tap into our intuition and open our spiritual eyes, all the wisdom and knowledge we will ever need to navigate this road will become available to us. The purpose of this book is to assist you in doing just that. My goal is to help you learn how to initiate and establish connections with your angels, and then to decipher their messages as you embark upon your spiritual journey.

Because connecting with the angels is such a highly personal and ever-evolving process, I chose to tackle this subject using a workbook format. While the first chapter of this book contains a basic overview and my thoughts on key aspects of angel communication, by the second chapter you are invited to get to know the angels on your own, through a variety of methods and approaches. The rest of the chapters expand upon this idea. You will be encouraged to learn about individual angels and discover how they appear to you, experiment with creating and utilizing a sacred space, and work with exercises and logs to track and reflect on your angel encounters.

This interactive approach seems more useful, to me, than asking you to simply read about angels. Doing that would have made me guilty of doing what so many other books do: imposing my own views, and the views of authors before me, upon your angelic world. In sum, this workbook is designed the way it is for a reason: so that you may compile and develop your own personal language with the angels. I've come to call this language the Angel Code.

The Angel Code is made up of icons, signs, and symbols that the angels use to communicate their messages to us here on the earthly plane. As I've said many times in my lectures as well as in my previous book, *Azrael Loves Chocolate, Michael's a Jock*, the angels will always speak to us in ways that we understand. The angels may connect with a musician through the notes of Beethoven's "Moonlight Sonata," with a painter through a vibrant self-portrait of Frida Kahlo, with a writer through the words of Maya Angelou.

While I believe that connecting with the angels can lead to a more meaningful and fulfilling life for you, I make no promises that it will improve your circumstances. After all, the angels are not here to fix your life, but to help you to navigate it using the tools that God has already given you.

I can, however, promise that through joy and sadness, triumph and turmoil, gains and losses, your angels will always be by your side, offering their unyielding support and comfort. No matter how turbulent the waters may be, God's messengers will always keep you buoyant—not to reinforce your faith in them, but to reinforce your faith in yourself. You are someone God trusts can weather any and all of the circumstances that come your way.

The time to connect with your angels is now. And don't worry, it's not as difficult as you may think. After all, the only thing you need is the desire. Then the high-speed data channels will burst open, allowing insight and wisdom to flow into your being.

So, let's plug in and ready ourselves for direct access to Heaven. Adjust your fire-walls, shut down all other programs, and let's begin streaming the one download you will ever need—the Angel Code.

ACKNOWLEDGMENTS

With deepest gratitude I wish to acknowledge:

God and the heavenly archangels for their continued love and guidance. I could never imagine my life without them.

All the cherished souls that create the beautiful landscape that is my life: my friends, readers, clients, students, and colleagues.

Llewellyn Publications for the glorious opportunity to live my dream as an author.

1

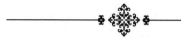

INTRODUCING
THE ANGELS

ANGELS ARE GLORIOUS AND MAGNIFICENT creatures. They have been walking beside us and interacting with us from time immemorial. History is brimming with examples of our fascination with angels, and there is not a single ancient culture or religion that doesn't incorporate some angelic archetype into its pantheon.

Why is this the case? Perhaps because humanity has always felt a deep-seated yearning to communicate with the Divine. And at the most basic level, an angel is God's preferred mode of communication. The word *angel* literally means "messenger." For thousands of years, angelic messengers warned people of impending floods, firestorms, and plagues; bestowed blessings; foretold riches; healed the sick; and announced the birth of great leaders.

But in today's world, the desire to connect with angels often seems limited to those who are religiously devout and/or New Age. Let me point out, however, that there's nothing particularly "New Age" about the angels. They've been weaving in and out of cultures for thousands of years! And just as angels are not necessarily "New Age," they're not necessarily "religious," either. As messengers, they do not belong—nor have they ever belonged—to any particular faith. Sure, Judaism recognizes a handful, Islam mentions four, and Christianity recognizes several (with some denominations acknowledging dozens). But the fact that religions involve angels does not mean that angels are merely "religious" creatures.

Take, for example, the experience of my spirit guide, Jake. He shared with me that within seconds of crossing over, the first angels he encountered were Raphael, Michael, Gabriel, and Cassiel. Jake was young at the time of his death, only twenty-eight, and had never put much thought into religion or spirituality when alive. So when he came face to face with these archangels, he froze in fear. He immediately confessed, "I'm not Christian."

Apparently, Gabriel arched his brow and cast a sidelong glance at his angelic brothers. He then returned his piercing gaze to Jake and shrugged. "Funny, neither are we."

"They always say that," one of the other archangels mumbled as they casually walked away. Stupefied, Jake turned his perplexed gaze to Cassiel, who had chosen to remain with him. This angel was dressed in street clothes, including a leather biker jacket and biker boots.

"Chill, man." Cassiel threw his hands up to stop Jake from speaking. "You're not going to Hell." All Jake could do was shake his head, to indicate that of course, he'd rather skip that area if he had a choice. He just stood there in complete awe of Cassiel … such a pure and luminous being, yet dressed as if he belonged in a goth rock band.

That's how I view the archangels in general. They're spiritual rock stars who happen to have incredibly long shelf lives. Everyone knows them. Everyone wants to see them, talk to them, touch them, embrace them. And while I think Archangel Michael invented the "rock star" concept (as he definitely has the persona for it), you don't have to stand in line at a holy shrine, repeatedly chant a prayer, or give offerings to get his autograph. Unless you want to. All the rituals and rites that we humans engage in are more for us than they have ever been for the Divine. If performing such tasks brings you comfort and the feeling of being closer to God, by all means continue what you're doing. Raised Christian myself, I've spent countless hours in prayer, often praying until my knees went so numb I couldn't stand up.

That was before I realized that my prayers were one-sided, however. I was doing all the talking and not very much listening. As Raphael told me years ago, "Everyone prays for answers, but no one sticks around long enough to hear them." I was very much guilty of that. I either prayed scripted words for hours on end, or quickly lodged my grievances before jumping up to go on with my day. After all, in my Pentecostal upbringing, I was taught to "take it to the cross and leave it there," meaning you didn't ponder your problems, you didn't worry about them, you didn't try think them out. You simply took them to God and let God handle the rest. This was a test of your faith.

Well, that kind of faith didn't get me far. I couldn't just blindly believe. I mean, how do I know that God even received the prayer? How do I know that my prayer isn't waiting in a queue behind six billion other prayers? Silly notions, sure. But long ago, I entertained them nonetheless.

Today, I prefer to balance faith with understanding and knowledge. Now, when I have questions for the Divine, I wait for the answer and pray that I'm receptive enough to hear it. If I'm aware that I'm not grounded, or if I'm caught up in a torrent of emotions, I usually say, "Get back to me as soon as you can."

Who am I addressing when I say this? Whoever is closest to the phone up in Heaven. God has many faces and many voices, so I don't discriminate among messengers. Cassiel, the Angel of Tears, is just as able as Gabriel, the Angel of Annunciation, to deliver a message.

Then again, there are moments when I'm in the mood for a particular angel. If I don't feel like being chastised for something I know I did wrong, I try to avoid Gabriel (like a child hiding to avoid a much-deserved spanking). I may call on Michael, who is always all smiles. Or I may cuddle up against Sandalphon, letting his playful personality rub off on me. Or I may call on Raphael, if I need a shoulder to cry on. But if Gabriel is the one who shows up, after my first reaction (a groan, since he is the most meticulous and militant messenger in Heaven), I take a deep breath and a moment of silence to prepare myself for a good thrashing of some sort. Then I surrender. "Okay, Gabriel, lay it on me."

What Angels Mean for You

In addition to their role as messengers, the job of the angels is to facilitate the manifestation of what Archangel Michael has called "God's Great Equation." Many of you might know this as "God's Plan." This is an important concept to understand before you engage with your angels.

So, before you go any farther in this book, ask yourself this question: *Why do I want to communicate with the angels?* Now, while this question may seem simple, the answer to it will determine how much long-term success you will have in engaging the angels. If you are looking to them to help you achieve the commonly sought-after goals of prosperity, health, love, family, and career, I suggest you close this book and take your money to a fortune-teller! Neither the angels nor myself are in the business of telling fortunes.

Likewise, the angels are also not in the business of making you happy. Will they offer comfort by being with you through your life's challenges? Yes. Help you find the love of your life? No. The angels are here to help you establish a lasting and productive relationship with the Divine, not to fix what you might perceive as a broken existence. Your life is exactly how it should be. If you are meant to have that perfect job with the 401k, you will. If you're meant to meet the perfect mate, you will. If you're meant to get your dream job, the angels will make it happen. Likewise, if you're meant get fired, the angels will make it so. The same goes for love and relationships, happiness and health, prosperity and wealth. The job of the angels is merely to help you understand *why* your life script has been written the way it has. They offer comfort and guidance that can help you in not begrudging your situation as much, if at all.

In sum, since our human existence has been scripted into God's Great Equation (God's Plan), the angels, in manifesting God's Plan, are here to help guide us on the paths we have set out upon. They are here to offer wisdom, to inspire, to lend their ears and shoulders when we're at our darkest hour. They are not matchmakers, brokers, job placement officers, or divorce lawyers.

One way to get out of the habit of looking to the angels to fix what we deem broken is to first set aside fixed ideas about what is *good* and what is *bad*. When we feel that life is going according to our agenda, when circumstances seem to be flowing in the direction we desire, we consider life good. When things are just the opposite, we consider life bad. But in order to make communication with the angels less of a headache—for us and probably for them as well—we have to understand that our celestial friends don't work in terms of what makes us feel good or what makes us feel bad, but rather in terms of what serves a purpose.

There is but one law in the cosmos that is inescapable, and the angels adhere to it to the letter: the Law of Causality. Cause and effect. Every action has a reaction. This isn't just a scientific theory—Jesus called it the Golden Rule, Buddha called it karma. And there's a significant chance that you yourself have said on more than one occasion, "What goes around comes around." The angels adhere to this rule and work to create the causes in our lives that will bring about a desired effect according to God's will; and like dominoes, the rotation between cause and effect moves on into infinity.

That said, there are no accidents in our existence. There is no such thing as bad timing or rotten luck. There's no such thing as too late, too early, too much or too little. Everything in our lives occurs exactly as it's supposed to occur. Everything. This is why I cannot overemphasize that the angels do not work according to what pleases or displeases us, or by what we consider good or bad. Those are all human concepts and perceptions—something that the angels simply do not adhere to. They have one focus and one focus only: purpose.

I know this may make the angels seem cold, callous, and detached from the human condition. But that couldn't be further from the truth. Every human is here in this reality because he or she chooses to be. Everything that occurs in his or her life is a choice that was made before birth—the pleasant, as well as the not so pleasant. The angels are here, as our brothers and sisters in spirit, to guide us along our life paths, and it is with love and compassion that they inspire, comfort, teach, and guide us the way they do. They know that human life in this reality isn't always enjoyable. Yet we humans always seem to come back here—and the angels walk by our sides, giving us what we need in order to get through our life lessons and the experiences that we've scripted for ourselves.

Before you can fully enjoy and utilize the relationship you establish with your angels, you must first own the responsibility for your life as the cocreator and coauthor of your circumstances. That includes the things that you feel you have absolutely no control over; before you were born into this world, you wrote down everything you wanted to experience in this lifetime. God approved it and trusted you enough to withstand it. The angels then moved in to help create the causes for events to happen. I know this may be difficult to believe, especially if you've suffered through a tragedy.

So, why would we choose to do something so seemingly insane? It's like I told a radio talk show host a while back who refused to believe he was responsible for all the tragedy in his life: when we are in the realm of spirit, we know that this life or this reality is just an illusion. We don't really get hurt—though we may feel it. We're not really poor—though we may look it. We're not really crazy—though we may act it. See, in the realm of spirit, we understand that none of this physical stuff matters in the grander scheme of things.

I liken this to playing video games. You can send your little character into a virtual war zone, but if he gets hurt, it's not that big of a deal. If his wares are stolen, oh well, you work at trying to recoup your losses. If he even dies, you can either bring him back for another round or create a whole new character. All in all, there is time and energy invested, but you know that the existence of that character is quite trivial when looking at the broader picture of your life.

Now, don't get me wrong. I'm not making our lives out to be as simple as a video game, because, unlike the video game, we can't turn this existence off. We can't just get up and leave life like we can the game console. And for some of us, we can't even get a brief breather to regroup! Once we enter this reality with our scripts, we have to go through with it. This may sound bleak, but understand this if nothing else—if God didn't think you could handle it, you would not be here.

So, we should actively keep ourselves in check, avoiding the spiritual snare of viewing everything as good or bad. Let such perceptions slip away to reveal what is truly important—the lessons we are here to learn, through this reality we have chosen to experience. The unrelenting coldness of the bank that has just put your house into foreclosure could be a lesson in not letting the attitudes of others affect your sense of self-worth, while the foreclosure itself is a lesson in detachment and impermanence—nothing lasts forever. The loss of a job that you had your heart set

losing Tigger a lucky

on lasting you to retirement could be a lesson in how to be more malleable and accepting of change. And the spouse who left you in the middle of all of this agreed to his or her role before you were born to teach you how to deal with issues of abandonment and betrayal.

None of those things are pleasant. We don't need psychic powers to figure that out. But through all of the trying experiences, we can gain more insight on life, as well as use the experiences to bolster our strength and faith in ourselves and the Divine. And while it may be difficult to deal with pressing life issues such as these, keep in mind that you are still in God's Great Equation—these experiences are also causes that will bring about other effects. You may read, several years down the road, that the house you lost was in a contaminated hot spot, rendering it uninhabitable. The job you lost may put you in a position to either take up employment with better benefits or encourage you to start your own business. And your spouse leaving you could have just opened the door for a mate who is better suited for you. It is because of possibilities like this that I encourage my clients—and often remind myself—to not begrudge difficult times, for they can and often do make way for better things.

This is where our connections to our angels come in. They help us process these experiences and learn our spiritual lessons, so that we are not blindly caught up in our egos, our pride, or our illusions of what we think life should be.

It is with this understanding that we should seek to engage our angelic guides. We should go to them for wisdom and encouragement, not pining for them to fix us or our broken lives. If we are supposed to be "fixed," we will be. The outcome is already set in motion.

Parent Angels and Mentoring Angels

As I mention in my book *Azrael Loves Chocolate, Michael's a Jock*, it's a common belief that guardian angels are appointed to individuals at the time of their birth. According to this belief, the guardian angel is supposed to protect the person from disaster or adversity or injury, or from sinning altogether. It's a comforting notion, isn't it? Knowing that Archangel Michael is watching your back every time you leave the house and venture into this cruel, cruel world can do a lot for your confidence, to say the least.

Well, as I discussed above, that's actually *all* that Michael is doing—watching your back. What befalls us in our existence has everything to do with what God has set in motion for us, and little to do with whether or not our guardian angels are sleeping on the job. When I work with clients as an angel intuitive, I try to discourage them from using the term *guardian angel*—because we tend to place a lot of weight and misallocated faith on this concept. Instead, I encourage the use of two other terms: *parent angel* and *mentoring angel*.

Your parent angel is in many ways similar to the stereotypical guardian angel. This is the angel who is with you from the time of your birth until well after you have returned to the realm of spirit. He (or she) watches over you and the progress you make in the course of a lifetime. This angel is ever-present, and facilitating communication with him or her will help you to discover and better understand your life's purpose. However, unlike the stereotypical guardian angel, your parent angel does not protect you from harm (as it is usually defined), unless it is God's will to do so.

I've received countless emails from readers of *Azrael Loves Chocolate*, each expressing how he or she resonates with one particular angel and its viewpoints or demeanor. Likewise, in the course of working with this book, you're going to quickly discover an angel you truly feel a heart connection with—one who not only makes you feel safe and secure, but whom you feel is like a close brother or sister, someone you can imagine yourself talking to on lazy Sundays while sitting on the front porch with a glass of iced tea. (Or not—Uriel and Cassiel aren't the type for that. You'd most likely enjoy their company sitting among the armory of their mansions or on a church rooftop overlooking a cemetery. To each his own!)

Now, whether or not your connections with the angels are always pleasant is another story. My parent angel intimidates the dickens out of me. And he knows it. Sometimes I can get sassy around him, but for the most part I'm usually tiptoeing past him, if not trying to avoid him altogether. Militant, with a tongue sharper than a polearm, he brings to my life the discipline I often lack. (I'm a slacker child of the 1980s, so I need my parent angel to kick me in the rear now and again to get things done. Procrastinators unite … eventually!)

I know that when he comes to the fore to talk to me, the subject will usually be one of a serious nature. At this point I cringe, bear down, and prepare myself to face another life challenge. Despite trying to dodge him, like I used to dodge my very strict father when I was young, I love my parent angel very much. We share the same views about the human world and I feel safe and secure in his presence. And when I do leave this physical realm, it is back to him I will go to review my life and discuss what it has meant for me spiritually. However, since many of you don't need a kick in the pants as often as I do, you will probably be much luckier and find great comfort in your parent angel.

The other angel that you will be working with—and at much closer range than your parent angel—is your mentoring angel. During angel consultations with clients, I focus on the angel or angels that I see in the foreground; these are the mentoring angels. If someone adores Michael but he's not mentioned in the consultation, I tell them not to fret. Michael may be their parent angel, whereas the angel offering guidance in the consultation is the mentoring angel, there to help with the life lessons that need to be learned at that particular time. When it's time to shift gears to the next lesson, another mentoring angel may step in.

Take my friend Lee, for example. Her parent angel is Uriel. In many ways, she mirrors this archangel's demeanor: she has a mind for philosophy and religion, a passion for justice and human rights, and a cynical nature; if she could help Uriel usher in Armageddon herself, she would.

"I'm so ready to pack up and go home," she often laments after watching too much negative news on TV. Like Uriel, she has a disdain for humanity's seeming inability to live peacefully, but nevertheless still strives to create harmony within her immediate world, hoping that it'll one day take root and grow. That's idealistic, maybe, but she's determined.

When I noted how much Lee's personality matches Uriel's, she immediately denied it: "But in the last reading you did for me, you said Gabriel was my angel." That's when I explained to her the difference between her parent angel, Uriel, and her current mentoring angel, Gabriel. We then made a small project of looking back into her past at distinct "seasons" of her life, to see which angels had been carrying her along in her life journey.

When Lee was a child, it was not uncommon for her Sunday school teachers to drag her out of class and take her to sit with her parents during the church service. She was far too probing and analytical for teachers and peers to handle, since she posed many philosophical questions. She quickly gained a reputation as the Sunday school menace.

"I got kicked out of Sunday school for asking if brothers had to marry their sisters, since Adam and Eve were the only two people God assigned to populate the world," she told me one day, smirking impishly over a cup of tea. "The unanimous *ewwww* by the other students, and then the awkward silence of the teachers, told me I'd never be welcomed in Sunday school again."

Keeping teachers and scholars—especially religious scholars, philosophers, and prophets—on their toes is one of Uriel's main tasks. If he's not engaging them directly, he's working through those like Lee, who have him as a parent angel.

Lee and I then went on to note how her interests and hobbies have changed over the years, and what was going on in her life during those times. As a young child, she was very sickly and spent many days at home, drawing pictures of unicorns and fairies or arranging star constellations on her ceiling.

"Daydreaming about mystical lands or exploring other planets was the only thing that kept me from being fearful about the many hospital visits I had to make," she said. Based on this, we could clearly see that Archangel Raphael, the Angel of Healing, was working in her life during that time, helping her cope by nurturing her imagination.

As a teen, Lee endured mental and physical abuse from her father. She also attended a school where she was the only minority student. The school made her feel very unwelcome. "I felt angry and alone, and the only place I could find peace was in a nearby cemetery. I'd sit there all day, just staring at the angel statues and mausoleums while listening to Bauhaus on my cassette player."

We could see that Cassiel, the Angel of Tears, was present during this period, working closely with her. He lends his shoulder to those who feel victimized and unjustly persecuted; and the cemetery, along with the darker "goth" influence, is definitely his signature.

As she became an adult, Lee battled with the stresses of balancing college and employment, and it was during that time that she discovered Eastern philosophies, which taught her about stillness and meditation. It was also during that time that she became active in environmental protection work. There is no doubt that Chamuel, the Angel of Nature and Enlightenment, had stepped in during this phase of her life, helping her find harmony while fostering her connection to Mother Earth.

At the time of our conversation, Lee was nearing her forties and had found herself at a crossroads in her life. When Gabriel showed up in her consultation with me, it was because she felt she lacked direction, and she was willing to surrender to the will of God and go wherever God instructed. When such declarations are made, Gabriel will offer guidance. He is the Angel of the Annunciation, sent to us to deliver messages and insight into our life's purpose.

So, as Lee's story illustrates, there is a different angel—a mentoring angel—for each season of our life. I'm sure that if you look back, you'll see where you had a Michael phase or a Sandalphon phase. But at the core, you're still much the same person, with the same passions and interests. Despite all the changes Lee went through, she never lost her interest in religion and philosophy, nor her desire to help bring peace to the world.

As you'll find while working with this book, the angels are highly consistent beings. Through keeping a log of what you're dreaming about, what you're focusing your waking hours on, or even what is attracting your interest, you'll be able to discern which mentoring angel is walking by your side. Each angel has an area of expertise, and his or her presence will not only bring you comfort during the lessons and challenges you encounter, but will also bring to light areas of your life that need attention.

Archangels Covered in this Workbook

As is indicated in various religious texts, *archangels* (such as Gabriel, Michael, and Raphael) are the angels specifically delegated the task of working with humans. They're also known as "Chief Angels." Although the title "archangel" is only mentioned twice in the Bible, other Christian texts (such as the *Book of Tobit,* the *Book of Enoch*, and St. Thomas Aquinas' *Summa Theologica*) list many angels by name, explaining angelic hierarchy and duties and relating stories of the angels' direct interactions with humanity. Of course, the definition and categorization of the term *angel* remains controversial among theologians; my best understanding is that although other "angels" (those lower in the angelic hierarchy) can deliver messages, they more often act as "helper" angels, dealing with elements of nature in the human world rather than with humanity itself. (It is also suggested that angels communicate among themselves, and some are tasked with interacting with human souls stuck between worlds, and with souls in other realms.) There is general agreement, however, that it is the archangels who communicate God's messages to us.

In chapter 3, you will find information about sixteen archangels. These are the archangels I've connected with, as well as established a personal rapport with, over my years working as an angel intuitive.

How, you may ask, do I actually go about meeting the angels? By a process I call *reverse angel-neering*. In essence, an angel initiates contact with me first, before I research his or her background. This is a validation method that I have been using for years now, and it's a wonderful faith-builder—I get to know an angel, and then find out that the books and scriptures support what I've already discovered. It's fun and inspiring. Reverse angel-neering also helped me shape the format of this workbook, since my goal is to help you build faith in yourself and your own intuitive abilities.

For the sixteen archangels in chapter 3, I list many of their universal traits or "associations" (derived from research and channeling). I then provide space for you to write down how *you* perceive the angel. Your list will probably include things that seem to differ from, or merely play upon, the traits I've listed—since how these universal elements *manifest* (in the angel's gender, hair color, specific items of clothing, etc.) may be different for each person.

Angelic personalities can manifest in a variety of ways because they come to us in forms that we are comfortable with. Like humans, angels will put on a different "face" depending on the particular person they're mentoring. Just as you may not be the same person at home as at work, with your friends as with your family, the angels shift their demeanors in much the same fashion.

I've learned from Archangel Michael that because angels appear differently to different people, throughout history people have assumed that the angel they've connected with is not the angel they've learned about in their religious lore, from other villagers, or from their spiritual leaders. Michael indicated that this is why there are so many names of angels—people thought that the angel they met was one who perhaps had never connected with humanity before. In reality, people just saw different avatars, or incarnations, of the same angels. But the list of angelic names kept growing. Language factored into this phenomenon as well, of course, as angel names bounced from one region to another.

Let's take a look at Archangel Gabriel as an example. Many of my readers think that I depict the Angel of Annunciation as being too stringent. (Heck, even Gabriel says I'm too hard on him.) But the side of Gabriel that is militant and commanding is usually the only side I see. Apparently, I'm comfortable with that.

Now, say you connect with Gabrielle, his female form. You will find her to be as comforting as a spring breeze and as tender as a loving mother. She never has a harsh word to say. Her voice is soft, her approach is nurturing, and she's always ready to wrap her large, billowing wings around you. You know those mystical, magical, glowing angels you tend to see on the front of angel books? Well, they're a perfect representation of Gabrielle.

my angel Gibrielle

But I get the snap-to-it, march-to-my-tune, do-it-or-else army lieutenant Gabriel, who has on more than one occasion said to me, "Suck it up, soldier."

Now, imagine this was a thousand years ago, and you and I lived in two different villages, separated by thousands of miles. This is before the invention of the printing press. This is before any reliable mode of long-distance communication had been established. How do we reconcile that the angel working in my life and the angel working in your life (at the same time) are both Gabriel? We couldn't possibly! The angels seem like two different entities, right?

And I'm sure that for many of you, your boss would say the same if he got a chance to peek into your personal life at home. Or vice versa, if your mother could see how you really are in an office environment.

At this point you may be asking, "Well, how many angels *are* there, really?" Scholars and theologians have debated the number of angels for centuries. According to various historical texts and religious authorities, there are only seven archangels—one for each of the seven heavens. However, these same sources differ as to who, exactly, these seven archangels are. Ultimately, based on my research along with what I have personally encountered, I must say that the number of angels and archangels cannot ever be accurately measured. Not only because there are too many of them, but because we'd have to first establish how to count them.

For example, if I talk to five different clients in the same day and all of them happen to have Gabriel as their mentoring angel, it doesn't mean that Jessica gets him on Sunday and Louise gets him on Tuesday. Gabriel can split into five Gabriels and walk with each client. And so this becomes our dilemma—do we count only one Gabriel, or all five? All of them are individuals who work independently of the Source angel. When the angel has served his purpose, he returns to his Source until needed again.

So, given an angel's ability to multiply, his ability to adjust his personality and appearance based on a person's comfort level, and the multitudes of languages in the world, you can see how we've ended up with more angel names than we can shake a stick at. Thankfully, each Source angel has a unique energy signature, which never changes regardless of how the angel alters his appearance, gender, or demeanor. This energy signature also remains constant throughout the angel's many avatars or incarnations. This workbook will teach you how to detect this signature, so that you will know which angel you're connecting with regardless of how he may appear to you.

That said, I don't recommend flipping through the pages just to pick a specific angel to work with. Let the angel pick you first, and then move forward to create and establish your connections.

A Note on Ascended Masters and Spirit Guides

I would be remiss not to note, here, that the heavenly hosts known as angels are not the only ones who can offer guidance and wisdom to those who earnestly seek it. For some of us, divine guidance may come from other (or additional) sources. While this book focuses primarily on connecting with the angels, you can certainly use the exercises and suggestions I provide to try to connect with your ascended masters and spirit guides.

Ascended masters are those beings who walked the Earth as humans and then transcended this reality after having acquired great wisdom and great knowledge of the spiritual world. The list of ascended masters is extensive and includes Jesus, the Virgin Mary, Buddha, and Kwan Yin. In New Age circles, this class of spiritual beings also includes gods from around the world and throughout history. I can personally attest that ascended masters may be figures whom many consider mythological—I have had encounters with Brighid, of Celtic lore; Pele, the Hawaiian goddess of volcanoes; and Diana, the ancient Roman goddess of the moon. This list of ascended masters may seem overly inclusive or fanciful to some, but as a child of the Creator I have come to know and appreciate the Divine's many radiant facets. And as a messenger myself, I must respect the beliefs of all those I connect with, as well as whatever incarnation God chooses to present himself in.

Spirit guides, meanwhile, are the souls of those who have lived a human existence and moved on, but who have not made a unique mark on history for their wisdom, spiritual leadership, etc. Your spirit guide could be anyone: a dear friend or relative, a cherished role model, even a beloved cultural icon. Your spirit guides are present mainly to comfort and encourage you—they possess an energy that you are already familiar with. However, keep in mind that these guides are still learning about both the human and the spirit realms, and may not have the understanding of the inner workings of these realms that the angels and ascended masters do. So, while it's perfectly fine to want to connect with your dearly departed Aunt Sarah, know that her role in your life is more for solace and support. The archangels and ascended masters are the ones who are better equipped to actually guide you through life's most challenging moments.

Communication vs. Connection

I believe that everyone has the ability to connect with the angels, ascended masters, and spirit guides. But because everyone is different, the biggest task is determining *how* each individual achieves this. If a person does not connect through clairaudience and clairvoyance, as I do, she may be proficient in dream work or clairsentience.

Although we're used to seeing angel books talk about "communicating" with heavenly beings, I prefer to refrain from overusing this word and instead use the word "connect" when possible. When people say "communicate," I believe it often evokes a mental picture of speaking directly to the angels. I must say that while not everyone may possess the ability to communicate with the angels, everyone certainly can connect with them.

That said, the fact that I use clairaudience and clairvoyance to connect with the angels does not in any way give me bragging rights. It's quite the contrary, actually. I'm such a skeptic sometimes, I have to hear, or see, or even feel my angel's presence in order to be receptive to his or her messages. You may be much more accepting than I'll ever be—dreams or perhaps the slightest intuition may suffice. Everyone is different.

The best way to establish a connection with the angels is to simply ask them to come into your life. If you actively seek them out, they will make their presence known to you. Approach them with a genuine yearning to connect, and the cour-   age to surrender to the understanding that you have not been, and never will be, in control of what happens in your life. Until you truly accept this into your heart, connecting with the angels is going to prove to be a daunting task, as you tussle between what you think should be and what actually is—according to God's will.

While we struggle to understand the notion that we're really locked in for the ride and there's no exit ramp until it's over, life moves on. The angels are constantly delivering divine insight and wisdom. I encourage everyone to approach the angels with an open heart, mind, and soul, for they will lovingly embrace you and guide every step of your life's journey. The key is to be willing to walk with the angels, no matter where they take you.

Nothing is in my control. Everything is already planned. I do see this now. I needed to be reminded.

2

OPENING THE
CHANNELS

THE FIRST STEP TO CONNECTING with the angels is simply having the desire to do so. Approach this new spiritual territory like a daring explorer on a new adventure, with an open mind and a willingness to go with the flow. In other words, I suggest that you don't approach the angels with the attitude that you already know a certain amount about them or even about yourself, but with the attitude that you know absolutely nothing at all. You want to be a blank canvas upon which they can paint a clear image of *what is*—according to God's will—without having to go through your conscious filters of *what should be*.

In a way, this process is like unlearning much of what you have learned about spirituality and even religion. I understand that doing this may be somewhat disconcerting for those of you who have grown up within constructs that teach us not to question our reality. But if everyone had obeyed those teachings, I wonder if civilization would have advanced as much as it has over the centuries. After all, if everyone had "played nice" and gone along with the program, as it were, we'd all still be swearing up and down that the Earth is the center of the galaxy and as flat as a pancake.

That said, letting go of preconceived notions about the world around you may be one of the most challenging obstacles you'll encounter when trying to connect with your angels, second only to surrendering. As much as I'd like to say there's a short-cut or ways around this, there simply aren't. At least, none that I've found. To put it bluntly, I believe it's either one or the other. Either you want angelic guidance, or you don't. If you do, then you have to meet the angels halfway. Surrendering to the will of God is the way to do just that.

Surrender. What is it, exactly? Is it about relinquishing control? Is it about taking leaps of faith at every turn? Yes. But do not ever make the mistake of thinking that surrender is an act of weakness. If anything, it's probably the greatest act of courage you'll ever undertake. It's about digging deep into your soul to find the strength you need to face all your fears. You cannot say, "God, I surrender, but don't take my job, my house, my family, my car, my friends…" Surrendering means that you accept that everything—*everything*—is a part of God's Plan for you. Pleasant or unpleasant.

When surrendering to the will of God, understand that to do so also means de-taching yourself from desired outcomes. How you feel a situation should be resolved and how the Divine views it are seldom the same. If you cling to the idea that "It has to happen like this! There's no other way," that type of thinking will build a wall between you and your spiritual guides faster than you can blink. Your angels' valu-able words of encouragement will get lost in this mental chatter. So begin training yourself now to quiet your mind, shed your desire for a particular result, and be open to guidance from above.

Keep in mind that the angels are benevolent and compassionate creatures who will guide you to where you need to be. They will never berate or belittle you, and they will never tell you to do anything harmful to yourself or others. Because it can be so easy for us to confuse the voice of the angels with the voice of our desires and wishful thinking, I always encourage everyone to test the voices and constantly seek validation of the messages you hear.

While surrender is the key to connecting with the angels, we must exercise dis-cretion and foster rationality as well. Just think about it—our world is plagued with powerful leaders who believe that God speaks to them and them alone, encouraging them to commit horrendous crimes against humanity. This is nothing new; humans have been mistaking the voices of greed and delusion for the voice of God for centuries. But God and the angels never told someone to steal another's land, enslave a nation, commit genocide, or subject the populace to tyranny.

While I believe that nothing happens in our world without purpose, the horrors of history were set in motion by people and needed no extra push from divinity. God knew what Hitler was going to do long before Hitler was even born, but the voices that pushed the tyrant forward in his grasp for power were nothing more than the voices of his own demented and psychotic whims. They were not the voices of the angels, those beings of light who work to illuminate the world with love and divine wisdom.

Even with this understanding, connecting with the angels still requires constant vigilance and a delicate balance between belief and common sense. It also requires us to be mindful that we are still bound by the Law of Causality. Every action we take has a reaction—every cause has an effect—in our world, and on everyone and everything in it.

Remember, I'm speaking from experience here. When Gabriel first appeared to me to announce the direction my life would be taking, I scoffed. In very polite words, I basically told him to go to Hell and take his announcement with him. What God had planned for me, and what I wanted to do, did not match up in any shape or form. I was young, but I had my mind made up as to how my life was going to be. I had a very clear vision about employment, education, and even retirement. And I wanted no part in what the archangel was trying to sell to me.

In a nutshell, he told me that I'd be helping others connect with angels and spirit guides, and assisting them in balancing their lives through that connection.

My instant response to Gabriel was, "I need something with a much more reliable paycheck."

You may gasp at my materialistic view, but let's be honest for a moment. Perhaps I can best make this point through a story—many of you may be familiar with the story in the Bible (Matthew 4:18–22) where Simon Peter, Andrew, James, and John drop their jobs as fishermen to become followers of Jesus. But now let's fast forward two thousand years, and imagine that Simon Peter and Andrew own a fishery in Boston. They have about forty employees. The company is successful, and they

have invested their lives and money into their venture. Their portfolios are diversi-
fied and lucrative, so they are feeling pretty confident that they can find wives and
support their families, put children through college, and later retire to Florida when
all is said and done. Meanwhile, James and John have a carpentry business in Phoenix that is going quite well despite the housing bust. They too feel they can finally
begin living their lives, now that they've put enough money away.

Then along comes this long-haired, tree-hugging, soft-spoken, intellectual community organizer who tells them that the plans they have made for living a life of financial comfort are all wrong. Instead, they should drop their businesses, chuck their
401ks, and join him on a cross-country tour to spread the news of a new kingdom
that is soon approaching.

Would you do it? Remember, you've got a mortgage, a car payment, a portfolio
to maintain, medical insurance premiums, etc. Are you going to drop all of that
and hop in a van, to drive across the country telling people to turn the other cheek
and love thy neighbor and refrain from judging others?

I don't care how many fish-stick sandwiches the community organizer could pull
out of his magic hat—there is no way I'd just drop everything I'd worked so hard to
get.

And that's what I told Gabriel. "Find someone else with less to lose."

A few months later, Gabriel found that person. He found her laid up in the hospital, paralyzed from a stroke, and quickly approaching homelessness.

That woman was me. Six months after his announcement, I had lost everything:
house, job, family, and health.

I no longer had anything to lose. And being unemployed, I had plenty of time on
my hands. When I first cried foul, just days after the stroke, Gabriel's only response
was, "You can come quietly or you can come kicking and screaming, Chantel." Either way, I was getting dragged along on God's Plan.

You think I surrendered then? Think again. I became more stubborn than ever
and refused to even talk to Gabriel at that point. Angered beyond words, I cursed
the heavens and somehow found enough strength one day to wheel myself out of
my hospital room and down to the chapel. For two hours I had the small chapel to
myself, and for two hours all I did was cry and curse and rock back and forth in my

wheelchair while plotting a way to wheel myself up to the hospital roof and plunge myself over the edge. I had never wanted death as badly as I did at that moment, and because I assumed I was going to Hell anyway for cursing God during my rant, I figured I might as well make my journey to the dark side complete and tell Jesus how I really felt.

"You didn't have to worry about a grocery bill," I said, glaring up at the crucifix. "All you had to do was wave your hand and voilà, instant seafood feast. You didn't have to worry about a car payment. You walked everywhere! And you never had to worry about a mortgage. Wherever you went, people gladly opened their doors for you, begging you to lodge with them."

I was infuriated, but this was the precipice upon which I'd arrived after running away from God for eleven years. No, Gabriel hadn't been the first to tell me what Heaven had planned for me. Jesus himself had come to me eleven years earlier, back when I was going to church as a born-again Christian. And as soon as he said, "You will teach, and you will heal," I packed my bags and got the heck out of Dodge. Fear that I might be schizophrenic (after all, I was hearing voices) and anger at my church over a very public but highly inappropriate purchase (a new Jaguar for the pastor when we were supposedly struggling with the "building fund") proved too much for me. I'd lost faith in my church, in myself, and in God. In that order.

For eleven years I ran. And then I ran right back into Jesus when I was more broken than ever. To say the very least, it didn't seem fair. When I vented my feelings that day in the chapel, I expected to go back to my room, mull over suicide a bit longer, and then just lie down and die. I had no family, very few friends who could help, no money, and no house. Nothing. I had nowhere to go once I got out of the hospital, and at that point I was convinced that the battle simply wasn't worth fighting.

What I didn't expect while sitting there in the chapel was to hear Jesus' voice again. After my colorful tirade, I felt sure he was going to wipe his memory of me and forget I'd ever existed. But he didn't. As gently and as lovingly as ever, he responded. I tried my damnedest to keep up my anger, but I couldn't. His presence diffused it almost instantly.

I still had a bit of a fight left in me, though. "You know, Lord, every time you send someone out to deliver a message from you, they get crucified," I explained. "I don't want to be crucified. I have a really low tolerance for pain." I rambled on, but then desperation welled up in my heart and I looked heavenward. "Why are you punishing me? I told you a decade ago that I didn't feel I was the right candidate for this." That was when I was still in college, unsure of what I wanted to do with my life. But JC wasn't backing down. In a most gentle and fatherly way, he reminded me of our conversation back then, and said that the purpose for which I was born had not changed.

Like everyone else in this world, I was locked into my destiny and there was not a damn thing I could do about it. That notion alone was more disconcerting than the notion that I might be bordering on schizophrenia, so I tested Jesus this time. "Prove it," I said. "Prove to me that this is really you and that I shouldn't just wheel myself up to the psych ward right this instant."

"Go back to your room," he said simply.

"And?"

"Just go back to your room. You'll see." And with that I felt his presence leave me, like a warm blanket being pulled away to expose me to the cold. With a sigh, I begrudgingly did as he instructed.

When I got back to my hospital room, my roommate's church members had shown up and were holding a Baptist revival that was loud enough to wake comatose patients. I tried my best to kick my wheelchair into reverse to escape the onslaught, but it was too late. One of the women had my chair by the armrests and was pulling me in, like a tractor beam on a spaceship. Resistance was futile, as the holy swarm surrounded me and held me captive. They instantly began interrogating me in ways that made Darth Vader look like Ward Cleaver.

"Looks like someone just had a talk with Jesus and ain't too much believin' what he has to say. Don't you think it's about time you started listenin'? Don't you think it's time you stopped runnin' all these years and just surrender and do what he put you on this Earth to do?" I'm sure the look on my face was a Kodak moment. It wasn't shock, but a narrow-eyed, smoldering glare that was directed out the window, as if Jesus was doing the moonwalk after having just scored a touchdown against my team.

I had never seen these women before, nor had I informed my roommate that I was going to the chapel. In fact, I had not even shared my personal problems with my roommate, as I tend to be quite private about such matters while in the midst of them. So, while the moment was hardly funny at the time, I've got a sneaking suspicion that those women were really Archangels Michael, Gabriel, and the gang in urban-fabulous drag, come to make my life miserable that day.

You may think that after something so profound and irrefutable, I would cast away all doubt and surrender right then and there. Nope. I was angrier than ever! I would have welcomed insanity over a miracle any day. My brain just couldn't seem to process what I had witnessed, and what I would continue to witness many times over. Miracles just didn't happen anymore, or so I thought. At the same time, after seeing the angels work in my life and other people's lives, I realized it was absolutely stupid of me to call all of it a coincidence. Regardless, I remained skeptical. Part of me is still skeptical, even to this very day.

Hey, what can I say? I'm stubborn! Then again, God knew I'd be that way when he put me here, and so I'm guessing that JC and the angels are expecting resistance from me at every turn.

Well, years have passed since that hospital room revival, and though I'm still of the mindset "I'll believe it when I see it," I have surrendered. I understand that everything that comes my way, everything that happens in my life—or doesn't happen—is already predestined. Sure, when JC or the angels come to me now, I question them and may even grumble a bit, but I acquiesce. After all, I've endured enough heartache and despair to last lifetimes. I'd be stupid to say no to the Divine ever again.

Now, I'm not telling you this to frighten you. I'm telling you this in hopes that you don't make the same mistakes I did. Then again, everyone's experience with the angels is going to be different. Maybe you're a lot more accepting of fate than I was. Maybe you're accepting of the angels but you're not quite there with the surrendering part. Or maybe you're so connected, you're sure that if you make a leap of faith, without a doubt God will catch you. I wasn't so convinced of that way back when, even when I asked Jesus if he'd catch me when I stepped off the edge. His reply: "You won't have to make a leap of faith off the cliffs. Just take the first step and I'll build you a bridge."

Trust me when I say, he has kept his promise.

And I don't believe that his promise was to me and to me alone, but to all of us. JC is just one of the many voices of God that speak to Christians, Jews, Muslims, Buddhists, Hindus, and everyone in between, including the nonreligious (which includes myself, even though I consider Jesus Christ the pillar of my faith).

When you first make the conscious choice to surrender, expect test upon test of your conviction. Don't beat yourself up if you falter, however. JC and the angels know well what it's like to be human, and they're here to help us, not judge us. They will support, comfort, and love you unconditionally, even if you're a stubborn nonbeliever like I have often been.

It is important for us to connect with the angels, I believe, because their very purpose is to guide and nurture the human soul. They are here to interact directly with us—not so much to reveal the mysteries of divinity, but rather to reveal to us the mysteries of everyday human life, to reveal our true human nature. Keep in mind that I am in no way implying that working with the angels will make your life easier. (If my story about Gabriel and Jesus isn't proof of that, I don't know what is.) To say the very least, I feel that my life struggles increased tenfold when I began working with them.

But then again, so have the blessings.

I believe that the closer you get to God, the rockier the road becomes. When you begin actively engaging the Divine, you will more than likely encounter more potholes and muddy ruts than ever before, which make your spiritual journey ever more laborious. The magnificence of the struggle, however, lies in knowing that God has not only equipped your car with the best struts and shocks, but that his Angelic Automobile Association is on call 24/7, to come to your aid whenever you need it.

Emergency Room Syndrome

Before I go into detail about ways to connect with your angels and guides, however, let me first cover something that will require your attention more than anything else—your attitude toward engaging the Divine. I've talked about this in many of my Angel Galleries. I wrote about it in *Azrael Loves Chocolate*. I've expounded upon it on radio shows, and I'm going to say it again, because this is one of the most common obstacles you'll encounter when trying to connect. I call it ERS—Emergency Room Syndrome.

We all know that prayer is one of the most basic ways to connect with God. Yet the thing about prayer, and any other forms of connection, is that people usually don't initiate conversation with their angels and guides until something happens—ranging from the slightly vexing to the full-out cataclysmic. While I try to drill into my students and clients alike the importance of surrender, I also try to reinforce the understanding that they don't need to *wait* until the world is crumbling down around them before opening up the channels to Heaven.

The most difficult problem that everyone across the board seems to have is connecting with the Divine when there *isn't* a crisis. Effective connections with the angels mean going to them when things are just peachy, as well as when things are a bowl of sour grapes. Go to your angels and guides because you love them and enjoy their company. Don't wait until something happens … or until you want something … or until you need something … to talk with them.

When people wait until their time of need, they're usually feeling uptight, upset, anxious, desperate, and all the other wrong things for connecting with the angels. At that point, they are looking for help—a desired result. They're not looking for a connection. In short, they are suffering from Emergency Room Syndrome.

This is how so many of us approach our angels and guides. We rush to our church or our sacred space, fall upon our knees, cry, plead, beg, and everything short of demand divine assistance. (Well, I've lodged demands, too, as I'm sure many of you have.) But when the going has already gotten tough, there's little room in our minds to actually take in the awe, wonder, and beauty of the archangels. Michael's usual sunny smile can do little to succor your desperation if you hardly know him. His telling you, "Don't worry, all will be well" won't help ease your fears one darn bit.

And how could it? Talking to him only when you're troubled is like trying to get comfort from an automated help line.

But if you take the time to talk to your angels on a regular basis and actually get to know them, their words of wisdom and comfort won't be lost on you. Once you've established that long-lasting relationship, the angels become like family to you, a family that has a vested interest in you and your life's purpose. So don't sell yourself short—connect with them as often as you can.

I'm not saying that Cassiel wants you to ask what his favorite goth rock band is or what his favorite Japanese dish is, though he'd get a kick out of it if you did. I'm saying that to go to your angels when you're not in a panic makes it easier for you to be receptive and accepting of their guidance when you *do* get in a crunch. So yes, the angels work well in a crisis. But why wait for a crisis when you can engage them and interact with them daily? Embrace them, and be inspired and encouraged by what they can do as companions along your spiritual journey.

While initiating contact with them, learn to trust your instincts and remember one fundamental fact—there is no such thing as right or wrong. You can't make mistakes doing this, as whatever you glean or discern was meant to be.

The angels work to further your life purpose only. If you interpret a twinge in your shoulder as a message that you should take on more responsibility in your management job, do it. If that decision leads to an unpleasant situation, it does not mean in any way that you were wrong about the message. For example, let's say you take on more work, which overburdens you in ways you didn't realize. You find yourself spending less time with your current love interest. You find that you don't sleep as much or that your stress levels are through the roof. You find your performance suffering so badly there's a risk you could be overlooked for the next promotion, or even lose your job altogether. You ask yourself, "How could I have been so stupid as to think the angels instructed me to go forward like this?"

Firstly, please know that you weren't stupid at all. You interpreted the message exactly how the angels expected you to. The point was never to propel you forward in that career, anyway, but to steer you in a completely different direction. Had the angels come straight out and said, "Hey, you need to leave this company," you'd have sent them packing, especially with all the years you've invested in your work.

So they took another route and now here you are, out of a job (and probably alone, too, since you ignored your mate for so long).

And this is exactly where you're supposed to be. These doors were closed so that other doors to other opportunities could open. You may be angry with yourself. You may doubt your ability to connect. You may even rue the day you met an archangel. (I know, I've been there myself.) But understand that the angels are here to create the causes that bring about God's desired effects. It's all about his plan, and the angels are here to guide you through it.

Eight Ways of Connecting with the Angels

There are various methods you can use to connect with Heaven's messengers. Many of them draw on extrasensory perception—ESP, or "the sixth sense" as it's commonly called. The exercises in this workbook will help you discern which techniques you may be strongest in, whether it's clairaudience (clear hearing), clairsentience (clear feeling), clairvoyance (clear seeing), claircognizance (clear knowing), or basic intuition. You can also connect through dreams and signs. All of these methods, in addition to other practices for contacting angels, are covered in this chapter.

It is a common belief in the New Age community that angels and spirit guides operate at such a high frequency in the spirit realm that it's difficult for them to connect with us for any extended period of time, hence making any type of connection difficult to establish. My thoughts on that? Hogwash. Once again, we have a case where human beings are trying to place limitations on something that has no limits—the Divine.

Now, while it may be difficult for Aunt Phyllis to connect with you after just having crossed over, it is not difficult for Michael to sit with you during a Super Bowl game and root for his favorite team. Aunt Phyllis could take a week, or a year, or your entire lifetime to acclimate to the spirit realm again, which is why you might not always sense her near. But for the archangels and ascended masters—the conductors of the cosmos—connecting with this world is as easy as breathing is for humans. It is not difficult for Sandalphon to sit and watch chick flicks with you. It is not difficult for Cassiel to go shopping with you at Hot Topic. It is not difficult for Iophiel to help you pick decorations for your baby shower.

By the heavens, I just can't emphasize enough that if we can't incorporate our angels into our everyday lives, how in the world can we expect to connect with them when we desperately need them? Ask Michael to your son's graduation party as well as to your evaluation meeting. Ask him to the park for your family reunion as well as to court for that speeding ticket. Don't wait until you're in trouble to connect with the angels. Invite them into your life every hour of every day, and soon enough you will find that connecting with them is just as easy as picking up the phone and calling your best friend.

So have at it! The following pages contain explanations of the various methods for connecting with angels, and then provide worksheets where you can experiment with the techniques. Remember that you may be stronger in some areas than in others, and that you may feel more comfortable with some techniques than with other techniques. This is to be expected. And most of all, remember that learning the Angel Code—how you, personally, communicate with your angels—takes time. But this itself is rewarding, since there will always be something new to learn when an angel comes into your life!

1. Clairaudience

(clair—clear; audience—hearing) The power or faculty of hearing something not present to the ear but regarded as having objective reality.

MERRIAM-WEBSTER'S DICTIONARY

Clairaudience is the method by which you hear your angels and spirit guides. The interesting thing I've learned about clairaudience is that you usually hear messages from the spirit realm in one ear only—usually the right. This isn't to say that the angels can't speak to you in your left ear, just that my personal experience, combined with that of my students and clients, indicates that picking up transmissions in the right ear is much more common.

You may be wondering, at this point, how you will be able to tell the difference between your inner voice (your intuition, your imagination) and the whispered words of the angels. The answer is simple: just ask! If you are connecting with an archangel, he will let you know. For example, when the idea for my Angel Gallery™ reading series first came to me, I was sitting alone at a teashop thinking about absolutely nothing. I heard the words "angel gallery," and right before my intuitive eyes, I began seeing how the event was to be formatted. After a moment I chuckled and said, "Wow, that sounds like a great idea! I'm glad I thought of this."

To which Gabriel drolly responded, "Yes, Chantel, we're glad you thought of it, too." Today, I tell attendees at my Angel Galleries, "If you enjoyed this, great. If not, lodge your complaint with Gabe—it was his idea."

And that's the truth. If you're engaging the angels and need to know whether they are actively connecting with you, they'll inform you. Moreover, you'll always feel that you're having a conversation with someone else, for an angel's tone and phrasing will be very different from your own.

That said, the voices of your angels and spirit guides will never—never—tell you to harm anyone or yourself, or to do things that go against the inherent good nature of your soul. They will always speak to you in a loving, supportive manner—even Gabriel and Uriel, as militant as they are.

For those of you who lean toward clairaudience, you'll quickly find out that each angel and ascended master has a distinct voice, even vernacular. For example, Archangel Michael's use of American colloquialisms and slang really sets him apart from the rest of the gang—and it also makes for some really amusing moments when he's talking to his brethren, who have yet to adopt contemporary speech.

Archangel Gabriel, the most stringent of the angels, won't wax Shakespearian on you, but you can still expect him to be very formal in his approach and talk to you like he's an army general.

Cassiel, Raziel, and Uriel are angels of few words, and will usually only speak if spoken to first. Even then, good luck on getting an audio response from them early on. Don't take it personally, however. If there is something they need you to know, they'll tell you.

Sandalphon and Haniel's voices are soft and have playful, boyish tones that can be quite comforting when they're not making wisecracks about their brother Michael. Sandalphon's twin brother Metatron and the sagacious Zadkiel, on the other hand, have deep, resounding voices (not too unlike God in the movie *The Ten Commandments*). Don't worry, it's not as intimidating as it sounds.

Chamuel, meanwhile, talks like a Hollywoodized kung fu master—softly and often in riddles. Raphael comes across as a wise old sage who prefers to tinker around with plasma orbs and the space-time continuum in his castle tower. His voice is deep and he speaks slowly, enunciating every word as if he's teaching a new language.

The ever-flamboyant Iophiel and the irreverent Ariel have voices that can coax the sun to rise two hours early. Bright, chirpy, and always up for a conversation about food, fashion, and festivals, Iophiel usually speaks a bit fast, and she has plenty of laughter to share with everyone. Don't be surprised if you get a case of the giggles when engaging her. Ariel is just as chatty, and is never short on snarky quips.

Ramiel and Raguel are masters at economizing both time and words. You can always count on them being succinct and straightforward. Idle chitchat is not their forte, so if you have a question, you can expect it to get answered, but don't expect them to lollygag by the water cooler. It's not that they're too busy for us humans, it's just their propensity for efficiency.

And then there's Azrael. One might expect the Angel of Death to have a voice that would instill fear in the most formidable of warriors. Such is not the case. Azrael has a deep voice that can be soft and comforting as well as effervescent. The Dark Angel has the most beautiful laughter I've ever heard. It's warm, hearty, and genuine, and in all the times I've connected with him, he's always been spirited and uplifting. While his job as the Angel of Death may seem grim, it is just that—his job. It does not in any way define him. Can he be menacing? Of course he can be. Dragging stubborn souls off to the spirit realm is not easy.

We have to remember that, above all, Azrael is an angel of compassion. He only goes to those who refuse to let go of this reality. For the most part, any angel can greet us at the time of death, but if we are desperately clinging to this world for all we're worth, with no intentions of detaching from it, you can bet that Azrael will be the one to show up. And as I've said many times before, you can go quietly, or you can go kicking and screaming. Until then, however, don't fear the reaper. It's perfectly fine to engage this angel on a regular basis, especially for those of you who have a fear of death or are dealing with notions of death, be it of a loved one or your own.

I think once you get to know Azrael, you will come to love him as I have and see him as a caring friend who only wants to help make our transition from this world to the next as painless as possible.

If you would like to experiment with clairaudience, see the exercise below. Before you start, look ahead to the pointers in chapter 4 about "Creating Your Sacred Space" (pg. 176) and "Grounding" (pg. 196). Also, you may want to photocopy this exercise for additional practice and keep your completed sheets in a binder.

∝ Clairaudience Exercise
Conversations with Your Angels

Compile a list of questions to ask your angel. The questions don't have to focus on a situation in your life; in fact, it'd be better if you kept the questions casual in this exercise. Remember, one of the keys to effective communication with your angels is to talk with them during times when you don't have a crisis that is in dire need of resolving. Keeping the conversation light and informal helps you to be more receptive to your angel's voice.

Make this a fun exercise. For example, ask Michael about his favorite music or what he thinks about a particular song. Talk about the upcoming football season or ask him to tell you a funny story about his angel brothers and sisters. Ask Sandalphon what he thought about the chick flick you watched last night, or ask Iophiel about ideas for an upcoming celebration you're planning. The point of this exercise is to see if clairaudience is one of your stronger abilities, and then to help you to hone the skill. So, asking questions that require a bit of elaboration in the answer will encourage you to do more listening and less talking.

The first part of this exercise contains questions about your experience as you make contact with your angel. Once that's completed, move on to the second part, where you will write down your questions *for* the angel and the angel's answers. At the end of your conversation, ask your angel to send you some kind of a sign, later on, to validate that it was indeed his voice you heard and not merely wishful thinking. Don't ask for anything specific—the angel will decide how best to communicate with you. What's important is that you request a sign. Whenever the sign manifests, return to this exercise to journal the experience.

Today's Date _____

How are you feeling as you begin this exercise today? Check all that apply.

- ☐ Angry
- ☐ Anxious
- ☐ Assured
- ☐ Cheerful
- ☐ Connected
  (in the present)
- ☐ Depressed
- ☐ Detached
  (wandering thoughts)

- ☐ Eh, I'm all right,
  I guess
- ☐ Fearful
- ☐ Frustrated
- ☐ Happy
- ☐ Hesitant
- ☐ Lonely
- ☐ Motivated

- ☐ Peaceful
- ☐ Skeptical
- ☐ Tired/Weary
- ☐ Uncertain
- ☐ Warm and toasty
  inside
- ☐ Worry-worn

MAKING CONTACT

1. Prepare your sacred space, relax, and ground yourself. Make sure that you are sitting in a comfortable position, and breathe slowly.

2. Voice your intent for this exercise. **Example:** *My intent for this session is to connect with my parent/mentoring angel and to practice my intuitive skill of hearing.*

3. Ask your angel his or her name and write it here: _____

   _____

4. What gender does your angel's voice sound like?   Male   Female

5. Describe your angel's voice in as much detail as possible (soft whisper, melodic, etc.).

   _____

   _____

6. Describe your angel's speech in as much detail as possible (fast, slow, contemporary, casual, formal, accented, etc.).

_____

_____

7. How does your angel's voice make you feel? (comforted, happy, curious, etc.)

_____

_____

Q & A WITH YOUR ANGEL

Enter your questions for the angel in the spaces provided.

Q1. _____

_____

_____

Angel's Response: _____

_____

_____

_____

_____

Q2. _____

_____

_____

Angel's Response: _____

_____

_____

_____

_____

Q3. _____

_____

_____

Angel's Response: _____

_____

_____

_____

_____

Q4. _____

_____

_____

Angel's Response: _____

_____

_____

_____

_____

Q5. _____

_____

_____

Angel's Response: _____

_____

_____

_____

_____

Validation Request

Ask your angel to validate this communication by sending some sort of sign. What sign does your angel say to watch for?

_____

_____

How are you feeling at the end of this exercise? Check all that apply and explain.

- ☐ Angry
- ☐ Anxious
- ☐ Assured
- ☐ Cheerful
- ☐ Connected (in the present)
- ☐ Depressed
- ☐ Detached (wandering thoughts)

- ☐ Eh, I'm all right, I guess
- ☐ Fearful
- ☐ Frustrated
- ☐ Happy
- ☐ Hesitant
- ☐ Lonely
- ☐ Motivated

- ☐ Peaceful
- ☐ Skeptical
- ☐ Tired/Weary
- ☐ Uncertain
- ☐ Warm and toasty inside
- ☐ Worry-worn

_____

_____

_____

_____

_____

_____

_____

_____

VALIDATION UPDATE

Date your sign manifested: _____

How did your sign manifest? Was it different than you expected? _____

_____

_____

Describe the experience. Where were you? What were you doing? etc.

_____

_____

_____

_____

_____

Additional Notes: _____

_____

_____

_____

_____

_____

_____

✳

2. Clairsentience /Empath

*(sentience—feeling) The ability to feel or sense something
not physically accessible by the five senses.*

MERRIAM-WEBSTER'S DICTIONARY

Clairsentience is the method by which you can feel the energy vibrations of your angels. I tend to toss clairsentience, empathy, and psychometry into the same pot when it comes to feeling the spiritual world around us. After all, those with this gift don't feel only the energies that the angels and guides emit, but can sense the spiritual energy of physical beings as well. It's an interesting gift, and one that I honed through learning the healing practice of Reiki—a practice in which a person can sense the flow of energies and vibrations in the body, and then facilitate healing by removing energy blockages and recalibrating vibrations to promote harmony and balance.

Everything has a vibration. Numerology (the study of numbers) focuses on the vibrations that numbers give off, which can be either harmonious or discordant. Astrology (the study of planets) talks about the vibrations that planets in our galaxy give off, which impact our personalities and our private lives, social lives, finances, and so on. Crystals and stones have vibrations. Colors have vibrations. Music has vibrations. Plants and wildlife have vibrations. And as a clairsentient—or empath—you will be able to pick up on all of this, in some degree or other.

Connecting with the angels in this manner can be a lot of fun, but for beginners it can be a little disconcerting. You may find yourself forever second-guessing whether that feeling in your gut is Michael telling you *no* to a question you just asked or merely the burrito you had for lunch. Needless to say, if you're planning to use this method to connect, be ready to practice, practice, practice.

When working with the angels and spirit guides, clairsentients will quickly find that their entire body is the conduit through which divine messages flow. From your earlobes to your pinky toes, you'll be a buzzing body of information, but the crux of it is to discern whether the ache in your knee is Uriel giving you a warning to stay still or just an old-fashioned forecast for rain. As with all methods of connecting, the angels will help you to calibrate your skill, but don't expect to be able to really compare notes with other empaths as to whether you're doing the right thing. Because you all feel things differently, the angels will communicate with each of you differently.

Long ago, I discovered that crystals and stones are a wonderful way to practice the art of feeling. For a classroom clairsentience exercise, I gave each student five different stones of the same size, shape, and texture—stones that physically felt as similar to each other as possible. I used carnelian, rose quartz, crystal quartz, jasper, and amethyst.

I then instructed the students to close their eyes and pick up each stone, feeling its vibration as I read off a list of words. The students were instructed to select a stone they felt best resonated with the words I dictated. I then wrote down the students' selections, after which I rearranged the stones for the students to select two more times.

Those who were strong in the area of clairsentience chose the same stone for the same word (carnelian for "sunny," for example) seventy percent of the time. Furthermore, of that percentage, about sixty percent made the same selections as each other. Meaning that not only did Kate choose carnelian for the word "sunny" each time I asked, but other students chose carnelian as well.

This experiment with crystals is fun to do with friends, and is detailed in Clairsentience Exercise 4 (Optional Group Exercise). Make an evening of it, and be sure keep the atmosphere light. Pressure to do or get things right can interfere with any method of connecting with the spirit world, so don't feel that it's all or nothing. After all, even I have off days—we all do. So take your practice in stride and let the angels gently guide you along in a way that only angels can, with full knowledge of what your potential truly is.

But first, let's practice a few solitary exercises (Exercises 1 and 2) to see where your clairsentience skills may be. Exercise 3 will guide you in connecting with the angels (similar to the exercise in the clairaudience section). Because these exercises are quite lengthy, it is recommended that you only practice one exercise at a time. Please be patient and try to reinforce your skills before progressing from one exercise to the next.

You'll notice that the exercises focus mostly on the hands, but as you learn to detect vibrations with your hands, the rest of your body will naturally follow suit, eventually allowing you to sense subtle types of psychic energy with your entire being. Where a clairaudient can receive an angel's message by simply listening to a voice, a clairsentient has to feel out a message through a hyperawareness of vibrational shifts around her.

Those with clairsentience will be able to glean messages and answers based on the emotions, mental images, and/or words that such feelings evoke. These exercises focus on honing the skill of feeling, or empathy, and serve as a journal to help you record, track, and validate your interpretations based on those feelings.

Before you start, look ahead to the pointers in chapter 4 about "Creating Your Sacred Space" (pg. 176) and "Grounding" (pg. 196). Also, you may want to photocopy this exercise for additional practice and keep your completed sheets in a binder.

❧ CLAIRSENTIENCE EXERCISE 1
Detecting Personal Energy

Today's Date _____

How are you feeling as you begin this exercise today? Check all that apply.

- ☐ Angry
- ☐ Anxious
- ☐ Assured
- ☐ Cheerful
- ☐ Connected
  (in the present)
- ☐ Depressed
- ☐ Detached
  (wandering thoughts)

- ☐ Eh, I'm all right,
  I guess
- ☐ Fearful
- ☐ Frustrated
- ☐ Happy
- ☐ Hesitant
- ☐ Lonely
- ☐ Motivated

- ☐ Peaceful
- ☐ Skeptical
- ☐ Tired/Weary
- ☐ Uncertain
- ☐ Warm and toasty
  inside
- ☐ Worry-worn

FINDING THE VIBRATIONS

1. Prepare your sacred space, relax, and ground yourself.

2. Voice your intent for this exercise. **Example:** *My intent for this session is to detect the energy vibrations moving through me and around me, and to practice my intuitive skill of feeling.*

3. Sit upright and comfortably in a chair with your feet planted firmly on the floor and your hands resting on your knees.

4. Close your eyes, and slowly lift your hands about three to five inches from your knees, keeping them palm down.

5. Very gradually raise and lower your hands from your knees to this height until you feel a shift in energy. You're detecting how far your aura—the spiritual energy field that surrounds you—extends from your physical body. You will

know when you've reached the threshold of your aura when you feel a sensation akin to gently breaking the surface of water or pulling apart two attracting magnets and no longer feeling their pull.

6. With your palms now facing you, try to detect the threshold of your aura again; remain just inside of it.

7. Lower your hands to the level of your pelvic bone and then gradually lift them up to the level of your belly button. You are now detecting the subtle shifts between your chakras, which are spiritual power points of the body. (There is more explanation about chakras in the meditation section in chapter 4, but for now you are simply determining your sensitivity to energy vibrations and documenting what you can sense with your hands.)

8. Return your hands to your lower pelvis and repeat going back and forth between there and your belly button, scanning for differences in how the energy feels between the two points.

9. Linger at your belly button a moment and then move your hands up to your diaphragm, slowly going back and forth to note the differences between the two areas.

10. Next, scan your hands between your diaphragm and the center of your chest. Linger at your chest and take three deep, cleansing breaths before proceeding; pretend you're infusing the area with love and warmth. This is just to help you clear your mind and relax a bit before moving on to the next power points.

11. When you're ready, move your hands up to your throat, and note the difference between the energy radiating from there and from your chest.

12. Progress up to your brow, alternating between there and your throat.

13. And finally, move your hands so they are palm down over the crown of your head. Move between this spot and your brow area to detect any variations between the energies that dwell there.

14. Take three deep breaths and slowly lower your hands to your sides, and shake them vigorously toward the ground to promote circulation and clear them of any residual energy accumulated throughout the scanning.

15. Repeat steps 7 through 13 and then answer the questions below ("Self Examination"). When those questions are completed, repeat step 14 above to end your session.

SELF EXAMINATION

1. When holding your hands over your lower pelvis (root chakra), what type of sensation do you feel? (magnetic, tingling, vibrating, heat, etc.)

   _____

   What does the sensation evoke? (particular words, emotions, mental images, etc.)

   _____

   _____

2. When holding your hands over your belly button (sacral chakra), what type of sensation do you feel?

   _____

   What does the sensation evoke? _____

   _____

3. Scanning your hands between your lower pelvis (root chakra) and belly button (sacral chakra), what differences do you notice?

_____

_____

4. When holding your hands over your diaphragm (solar plexus chakra), what type of sensation do you feel?

_____

What does the sensation evoke? _____

_____

5. Scanning your hands between your belly button (sacral chakra) and diaphragm (solar plexus chakra), what differences do you notice?

_____

_____

6. When holding your hands over the center of your chest (heart chakra), what type of sensation do you feel?

_____

What does the sensation evoke? _____

_____

7. Scanning your hands between your diaphragm (solar plexus chakra) and the center of your chest (heart chakra), what differences do you notice?

_____

_____

8. When holding your hands over your throat (throat chakra), what type of sensation do you feel?

_____

What does the sensation evoke? _____

_____

9. Scanning your hands between the center of your chest (heart chakra) and throat (throat chakra), what differences do you notice?

_____

_____

10. When holding your hands over your brow (third eye chakra), what type of sensation do you feel?

_____

What does the sensation evoke? _____

_____

11. Scanning your hands between your throat (throat chakra) and brow (third eye chakra), what differences do you notice?

_____

_____

12. When holding your hands over the top of your head (crown chakra), what type of sensation do you feel?

_____

What does the sensation evoke? _____

_____

13. Scanning your hands between your brow (third eye chakra) and the top of your head (crown chakra), what differences do you notice?

_____

_____

MORE PRACTICE (CHOOSE ANY TWO CHAKRAS)

Scanning your hands between your _____ (_____chakra)

and _____ (_____chakra), what differences do you note?

_____

_____

Scanning your hands between your _____ (_____chakra)

and _____ (_____chakra), what differences do you note?

_____

_____

How are you feeling at the end of this exercise? Check all that apply and describe.

☐ Angry
☐ Anxious
☐ Assured
☐ Cheerful
☐ Connected
  (in the present)
☐ Depressed
☐ Detached
  (wandering thoughts)

☐ Eh, I'm all right,
  I guess
☐ Fearful
☐ Frustrated
☐ Happy
☐ Hesitant
☐ Lonely
☐ Motivated

☐ Peaceful
☐ Skeptical
☐ Tired/Weary
☐ Uncertain
☐ Warm and toasty
  inside
☐ Worry-worn

_____

_____

_____

_____

ᴄ Clairsentience Exercise 2
Detecting Crystal Energy

For this exercise you will need seven to ten polished crystals or stones, measuring from 2 cm to 3 cm. All the stones must be as close in size, shape, and texture as possible. The stones must also be cleansed and programmed (see the "Crystals and Gemstones" section in chapter 4). You will also need a small pouch or box to hold your stones.

Each time you practice this exercise you are only going to use five of your stones, but try to create a new combination of stones as often as possible.

Today's Date _____

How are you feeling as you begin this exercise today? Check all that apply.

- ☐ Angry
- ☐ Anxious
- ☐ Assured
- ☐ Cheerful
- ☐ Connected (in the present)
- ☐ Depressed
- ☐ Detached (wandering thoughts)

- ☐ Eh, I'm all right, I guess
- ☐ Fearful
- ☐ Frustrated
- ☐ Happy
- ☐ Hesitant
- ☐ Lonely
- ☐ Motivated

- ☐ Peaceful
- ☐ Skeptical
- ☐ Tired/Weary
- ☐ Uncertain
- ☐ Warm and toasty inside
- ☐ Worry-worn

Finding the Vibrations

1. Prepare your sacred space, relax, and ground yourself. Make sure you are sitting in a comfortable position and breathe slowly.

2. Voice your intent for this exercise. **Example:** *My intent for this session is to detect the energy vibrations moving through me and around me, and to practice my intuitive skill of feeling.*

3. Close your eyes and withdraw five stones from the pouch. Set them on the table before you and arrange them in a row about three to four inches apart.

4. Similar to the aura detection process in Exercise 1, you are now going to use the index and middle fingers of your dominant hand to detect the aura threshold of each stone. (Rest your opposite hand on your knee.) Begin by lightly touching the leftmost stone, Stone #1, and then gradually lifting your fingers away until you feel that you have moved outside of the stone's energy field. Repeat this with the other four stones and note if the aura sizes and intensity differ from stone to stone.

5. After examining all five stones, return to your first stone to detect its aura threshold again, remaining just inside of it. You will now begin scanning the stones as you scanned your chakras in Exercise 1, noting differences in the stones' vibrations.

6. When you complete scanning, drop your hands to your sides and shake them vigorously toward the ground to encourage circulation and clear them of any residual energy from the stones. Relax and take three deep breaths.

7. Repeat step 5 and answer the questions below. When the questions are completed, repeat step 6 to end your session.

SELF EXAMINATION

List your stones in order from left to right.

Stone #1 _____

Stone #2 _____

Stone #3 _____

Stone #4 _____

Stone #5 _____

1. When holding your hand over Stone #1, what type of sensation do you feel? (magnetic, tingling, vibrating, heat, etc.)

   _____

   What does the sensation evoke? (particular words, emotions, mental images, etc.)

   _____

   _____

2. When holding your hand over Stone #2, what type of sensation do you feel?

   _____

   What does the sensation evoke? _____

   _____

3. Scanning your hand between Stone #1 and Stone #2, what differences do you notice?

   _____

   _____

4. When holding your hand over Stone #3, what type of sensation do you feel?

   _____

   What does the sensation evoke? _____

   _____

5. Scanning your hand between Stone #2 and Stone #3, what differences do you notice?

_____

_____

6. When holding your hand over Stone #4, what type of sensation do you feel?

_____

What does the sensation evoke? _____

_____

7. Scanning your hand between Stone #3 and Stone #4, what differences do you notice?

_____

_____

8. When holding your hand over Stone #5, what type of sensation do you feel?

_____

What does the sensation evoke? _____

_____

9. Scanning your hand between Stone #4 and Stone #5, what differences do you notice?

_____

_____

MORE PRACTICE (CHOOSE ANY TWO STONES)

Scanning your hand between Stone #_____ and Stone #_____, what differences do you notice?

_____

_____

Scanning your hand between Stone #_____ and Stone #_____, what differences do you notice?

_____

_____

How are you feeling at the end of this exercise? Check all that apply and describe.

- ☐ Angry
- ☐ Anxious
- ☐ Assured
- ☐ Cheerful
- ☐ Connected (in the present)
- ☐ Depressed
- ☐ Detached (wandering thoughts)

- ☐ Eh, I'm all right, I guess
- ☐ Fearful
- ☐ Frustrated
- ☐ Happy
- ☐ Hesitant
- ☐ Lonely
- ☐ Motivated

- ☐ Peaceful
- ☐ Skeptical
- ☐ Tired/Weary
- ☐ Uncertain
- ☐ Warm and toasty inside
- ☐ Worry-worn

_____

_____

_____

_____

_____

⚘ CLAIRSENTIENCE EXERCISE 3
Sensations of Your Angels

Compile a list of questions to ask your angel. These questions should focus on helping you to get to know him or her, as well as helping you to become familiar with the angel's vibrations. Make this a fun project and keep the questions casual and lighthearted. Remember, learning to connect with angels when you're not in the midst of a crisis helps you to be more receptive to their presence when a stressful situation arises.

Today's Date _____

How are you feeling as you begin this exercise today? Check all that apply.

☐ Angry

☐ Anxious

☐ Assured

☐ Cheerful

☐ Connected
  (in the present)

☐ Depressed

☐ Detached
  (wandering thoughts)

☐ Eh, I'm all right,
  I guess

☐ Fearful

☐ Frustrated

☐ Happy

☐ Hesitant

☐ Lonely

☐ Motivated

☐ Peaceful

☐ Skeptical

☐ Tired/Weary

☐ Uncertain

☐ Warm and toasty
  inside

☐ Worry-worn

MAKING CONTACT

1. Prepare your sacred space, relax, and ground yourself.

2. Voice your intent for this exercise. **Example:** *My intent for this session is to connect with my parent/mentoring angel and to practice my intuitive skill of feeling.*

3. Sit upright and comfortably in a chair with your feet planted firmly on the floor and your hands resting on your knees, palms up.

4. Close your eyes and concentrate on your breathing. Allow yourself to relax and shift your focus to your hands. How do they feel? Warm, cool? Can you feel your own pulse in your palms or a slight buzzing? Can you feel the air flowing over them? Linger in the moment for a few minutes.

5. When you feel you are ready, ask your angel to connect with you, keeping in mind the following points. At the end of your session, ask your angel to send you a sign, later, to validate his presence. Write it down. Whenever it manifests, return to this exercise to journal the experience.

6. First, turn your attention to your hands. In which hand do you feel a shift in vibrations the most? (circle the best answer)   Right   Left   Same

7. Is a name coming to you?   Yes   No

   a. If yes, write your angel's name here: _____

   b. Explain how the name came to you (you heard it, saw it, etc.).

   _____

   _____

   _____

8. What does your angel's presence feel like? (magnetic, tingling, vibrating, heat, etc.)

   _____

9. What does the sensation you felt in the previous question evoke? (particular words, emotions, mental images, etc.)

   _____

   _____

10. Based on what you're feeling, describe your angel (gender, demeanor, appearance, etc.).

_____

_____

Q & A WITH YOUR ANGEL

Enter your question for the angel in the spaces provided.

Q1. _____

_____

_____

Angel's Response (explain the vibrations you sense, where you feel them, what they evoke, and your interpretation): _____

_____

_____

_____

_____

_____

Q2. _____

_____

_____

Angel's Response: _____

_____

_____

_____

_____

Q3. _____

_____

_____

Angel's Response: _____

_____

_____

_____

_____

Q4. _____

_____

_____

Angel's Response: _____

_____

_____

_____

_____

VALIDATION REQUEST

Ask your angel to validate this communication by sending some sort of sign. What sign does your angel say to watch for?

_____

_____

How are you feeling at the end of this exercise? Check all that apply and describe.

- ☐ Angry
- ☐ Anxious
- ☐ Assured
- ☐ Cheerful
- ☐ Connected (in the present)
- ☐ Depressed
- ☐ Detached (wandering thoughts)

- ☐ Eh, I'm all right, I guess
- ☐ Fearful
- ☐ Frustrated
- ☐ Happy
- ☐ Hesitant
- ☐ Lonely
- ☐ Motivated

- ☐ Peaceful
- ☐ Skeptical
- ☐ Tired/Weary
- ☐ Uncertain
- ☐ Warm and toasty inside
- ☐ Worry-worn

_____

_____

_____

_____

_____

_____

VALIDATION UPDATE

Date your sign manifested: _____

How did your sign manifest? Was it different than you expected? _____

_____

_____

Describe the experience. Where were you? What were you doing? etc.

_____

_____

_____

_____

_____

Additional Notes: _____

_____

_____

_____

_____

_____

CLAIRSENTIENCE EXERCISE 4
(OPTIONAL GROUP EXERCISE)
Detecting Crystal Energy

This is a fun and engaging activity to do with friends and family. Be sure to keep the atmosphere light and playful.

For this exercise, each person will need one of each: rose quartz, crystal quartz, hematite, carnelian, and amethyst. All the stones should be polished, measuring from 2 cm to 3 cm, and should also be as close in size, shape, and texture as possible. The stones must be cleansed and programmed (see the "Crystals and Gemstones" section in chapter 4).

1. Prepare the space where you are working the same way you would prepare your sacred space, smudging or offering a prayer to promote harmony and encourage camaraderie among participants.

2. Select a group leader to arrange stones in front of the participants. For convenience, all participants should be sitting at a table with enough space to set their stones before them.

3. Group Leader: Instruct participants to close their eyes and keep them closed for the remainder of the exercise.

   a. Group Leader: Arrange each participant's stones in a row and within the participant's reach. The order in which the stones are placed for each participant is not important.

   b. Group Leader: Instruct the participants to gently locate their stones on the table in front of them. Once everyone is comfortable and able to locate all five stones, you can read off a list of words and instruct each participant to select a stone that they feel best describes the word. Record your results on a pre-made chart similar to the sample provided below. (Use this workbook's section on "Crystals and Gemstones," as well as the chapter on "Angel Associations," to help you compile a list of word/stone associations.)

Word	Commonly Associated Stone	Amy	Sheila	Meghan
Sunshine	Carnelian & Crystal Quartz	*Carnelian*	*C. Quartz*	*Carnelian*
Love	Rose Quartz	*Amethyst*	*Rose Quartz*	*Rose Quartz*
Tranquility	Rose Quartz & Amethyst	*Rose Quartz*	*Carnelian*	*Hematite*
Strength	Hematite	*Hematite*	*Carnelian*	
Dreams	Amethyst			
Movement	Carnelian			
Stillness	Hematite			
Courage	Carnelian			
Air	Amethyst & Crystal Quartz			

c. Group Leader: When you complete the exercise, instruct participants to drop their hands to their sides and shake them vigorously toward the ground, to promote circulation and clear them of any residual energy from the stones.

d. Group Leader: Ask the participants to relax and take three deep breaths. Instruct them to open their eyes, and then begin a discussion about the results of the exercise. Remember, there are no wrong or right answers because people interpret words differently (for the word "Tranquility" in the chart above, Amy chose rose quartz because she equates love with tranquility; Sheila chose carnelian because sunlight makes her feel peaceful; and Meghan chose hematite because she associates strength and stillness with a state of calm). Since this is a time for togetherness and sharing in a spiritual atmosphere, encourage dialogue between participants and ask them what they experienced while connecting to the stones' energy and how they feel about the exercise results.

VARIATION

Instead of using crystals, have each participant place a small personal item in a box (keys, mirror, brush, pen, etc.). This should be done in a way that no other participants can see or know who the item belongs to.

Group Leader:

1. Place the items in the center of the table. Select one item at a time and ask participants to write down the type of vibrations they feel from the object, as well as the name of the person whom they believe owns the object.

2. Once all the items are examined, take turns discussing each object, but ask that everyone keep their guess about the object's owner secret until the end of the session.

3. Have everyone collect their item and then have everyone reveal their guesses to see who was correct.

3. Clairvoyance

*(voyance—seeing) 1: the power or faculty of discerning
objects not present to the senses 2: ability to perceive matters
beyond the range of ordinary perception.*

MERRIAM-WEBSTER'S DICTIONARY

While connecting with the angels may be a bit difficult for many of you in the beginning, regardless of the method you choose, I believe that going the clairvoyant route may prove the most daunting choice of all. As I explain in the "Meditation in Your Sacred Space" section in chapter 4, not everyone can visualize or "see" images in their mind. Because clairvoyance significantly depends on this ability, some of you may struggle with it.

In my years of talking with people about angels, I've learned that everyone *wants* to see an angel—to which I often reply, "So do I!" That statement may confuse you a little, but trust me, I'm not being a smart aleck! It's just that everyone believes I see the angels with my physical eyes. My God, wouldn't I love to, but it just doesn't work that way for me. At least, not often.

The only angel I've seen with my physical eyes is Cassiel, and he darn near scared the bejesus out of me. I was young, in my early twenties, when he decided to visit. The moon was full, and shining so brightly into my bedroom window that I could read by its beautiful blue light. As I was preparing for bed, I spotted him there in the corner of my room. At first I thought it was my spirit guide, Jake, as the two have an uncanny resemblance. But I could tell from Cassiel's aura that he was no former human.

At the time I wasn't actively connecting with angels, just with my spirit guide. I had read about Cassiel, however, and Jake had introduced me to the angel in a meditation several months prior; but as with all things spiritual, I was leery—especially of an archangel dressed in black from head to toe: a black muscle shirt, faded jeans, combat boots, and a trench coat. Cass looked nothing like an angel to me, but still, his divine radiance got past my defenses. I didn't invite him into my life right at that moment, but I didn't scream "Get thee behind me, Satan!" either.

Nevertheless, his appearing to me in this fashion was nothing if not completely alarming. I was frozen in place, and for a millisecond I wondered if seeing him with my physical eyes was an omen of death (especially given the way he dresses).

"You're not dying." His silvery gray eyes shimmered at me from across the room. I slowly nodded and took a deep breath, peering at him. He seemed solid enough, and even cast a shadow on the wall behind him.

"So … why are you here?" I asked.

"I just wanted to let you know that your dad says hi." He smiled a sad smile, and a lump welled in my throat. It had been months since my father had passed away, and at the time I was a lot like my mother—I had a hardened core that didn't allow emotions to cripple me. He died; I wept; it was over. Father was gone and no amount of mourning was going to bring him back. Cassiel's words, however, stunned me, and tears instantly flooded my heart and made their way down my cheeks. It was the last thing I'd expected to hear.

"Thanks." My voice hitched and I covered my face, angry that my reaction was so immediate.

"I'm here when you decide to let me in," Cassiel whispered in my ear, and I felt his hand on my shoulder. When I looked up again, he was gone. But he left behind such a profound sense of warmth, peace, and security that I wasted no time inviting him back. I wanted to learn more about him and his relationship with God, and what his presence in my spiritual world would mean.

Other than that occurrence, I've only seen Cassiel out the corner of my eye, usually standing in the shadows or sitting in a moonlit tree. And as with most apparitions—or with one's imagination—turning my gaze in his direction meant that I would see nothing at all, since he would instantly vanish.

You may wonder why I just mentioned "one's imagination," as it seems to imply that what I saw wasn't real. We could open a debate about what "real" truly means, of course, but that's another book for another time. In this case, I mention the imagination because it is by far the most useful tool you can possess when meditating or engaging in clairvoyance. The imagination is a bridge to the inner voice, your intuition. By letting go of preconceived notions and entertaining the miraculous possibilities that can result through connecting with your angels, you are putting yourself in a place of surrender, a place where the mind and soul are open to experiencing what you may have at one point thought impossible. By allowing your imagination to flow, you are engaging in the creative processes of the universe. Because you are moving away from the obstacles of conditioned thought and expectations, you are moving yourself ever closer to direct alignment with the Creator.

Your imagination allows you to tap into your intuitive energies, which in turn fuel your meditative—as well as clairvoyant—abilities. If you can visualize the angels, then you can connect with them. At first you may only be able to see your angels in meditation. Some of you may also encounter what several of my clients call "silent angels"—"I can see Michael as clear as day in my visions, but he won't talk to me!" they say. When I get complaints of this nature, I sort of smirk and say, "Did you plug your earphones in?" At that point, my clients often cant their heads and give me a blank stare.

They were going for clairvoyance, and they got it. Now, if they want sound with that, they'd best get to practicing clairaudience. Intuitive tools don't always come to us like technology. Not everyone can experience the high-definition television set with surround sound. Some of us will get images only. Some of us will get sound only. Some of us may get the images, the sound, and the interactive features as well. What you get depends on what you signed up for in your contract with God for this lifetime. The point is to be grateful for what you have, and not begrudge what you don't have.

While I now take it for granted that I am clairaudient, clairsentient, and clairvoyant, I've found myself to be seriously lacking in the claircognizant arena. At first I was snippy about this, but hey, three outta four ain't bad. One out of four isn't bad, either. So before you start banging on your television set wondering why you're not getting sound with your picture, try to remember why: simply put, your learning style is more visual than auditory. But that does not mean you are any less capable than the next person of receiving messages.

You'll just have to read lips. No, I'm kidding.

You won't have to learn how to read lips (though now that I think about it, it might not be such a bad idea—someone try it out and get back to me on how it works). In the meantime, though, you'll have to learn how to read your angels' body language to get clues into the messages they're conveying. Luckily, the angels are happy to supply other visual cues to help you along. For numerous examples of body language and visual cues, please see the "Helpful Hints for Using Clairvoyance and Dreams" section at the end of this chapter (pg. 115). You can consult chapter 3, as well, for icons and images commonly associated with specific angels.

A quick note, though, before you commit such images to memory. If I've said it once, I've said it a thousand times (no exaggeration): the angels speak to us in languages we understand. What I've listed in this workbook is based on what the symbols have generally meant for *me*, along with what I've gleaned from talking with students and clients. For me, a pink rose has always meant a mother's love or divine love. However, if somewhere in your past pink roses were attached to a very unpleasant situation, the angels may not use that image for you, and instead choose another one.

It's because of these variables that working with the intuition can never be an exact science. As the skeptic I am, I wish there were substantial scientific data to support metaphysics. But such is not the case, and each and every one of us is basically left with trial and error as we journey down the intuitive road. As I've mentioned, the format of this book reflects this view—since what I've experienced and what you will experience could be two different things. In essence, I'm just showing you where to start your journey. You're the one who ultimately has to fill in the map.

In chapter 4, you will find a detailed walkthrough meditation designed to help you connect with the angels. Of course, once you've established your connections, you may no longer need to use meditation to see your angels. Instead, you may simply be able to close your eyes and instantly get results. Better yet, you may eventually arrive at a point where you will be able to see your angels even with your physical eyes wide open.

If you would like to experiment with clairvoyance, I encourage you to browse the "Helpful Hints for Using Clairvoyance and Dreams" section (pg. 115) before or soon after you do the exercise below. Before you start, look ahead to the pointers in chapter 4 about "Creating Your Sacred Space" (pg. 176) and "Grounding" (pg. 196). Also, you may want to photocopy this exercise for additional practice and keep your completed sheets in a binder.

⤬ CLAIRVOYANCE EXERCISE
Visions of Your Angels

Compile a list of questions to ask your angel. These questions should focus on familiarizing yourself with his appearance and icons. You're getting to know your angel on a personal level, so have fun with this. The more familiar you are with your angel, the more receptive you'll be to his manifestation, and to messages he sends during stressing times.

Today's Date _____

How are you feeling as you begin this exercise today? Check all that apply.

☐ Angry
☐ Anxious
☐ Assured
☐ Cheerful
☐ Connected
  (in the present)
☐ Depressed
☐ Detached
  (wandering thoughts)

☐ Eh, I'm all right,
  I guess
☐ Fearful
☐ Frustrated
☐ Happy
☐ Hesitant
☐ Lonely
☐ Motivated

☐ Peaceful
☐ Skeptical
☐ Tired/Weary
☐ Uncertain
☐ Warm and toasty
  inside
☐ Worry-worn

MAKING CONTACT

1. Prepare your sacred space, relax, and ground yourself. Make sure that you are sitting in a comfortable position, and breathe slowly.

2. Voice your intent for this exercise. **Example:** *My intent for this session is to connect with my parent/mentoring angel and to practice my intuitive skill of seeing.*

3. Close your eyes and concentrate on your breathing. Allow yourself to relax and shift your attention to the center of your brow, commonly called the third eye. It is through this eye that you will peer into the realm of spirit to see your angel.

4. Ask your angel to allow you to see him, so that you may connect with him and receive his guidance.

5. When your angel reveals his presence to your mind's eye, examine his form and appearance, keeping in mind the following points. At the end of your session, ask your angel to send you a sign, later, to validate his presence. Write it down. Whenever it manifests, return to this exercise to journal the experience.

6. Ask your angel his or her name, and write it here: _____

7. In what way did he reveal his name to you? (presented a scroll, wrote on a blackboard, etc.).

_____

8. What gender does your angel appear to be?   Male   Female

9. Describe your angel's appearance in as much detail as possible (clothing, build, etc.).

_____

_____

10. Describe any icons your angel may have been holding when he appeared (sword, scroll, roses, etc.).

_____

_____

11. How does your angel's appearance make you feel? (comforted, happy, curious, etc.)

_____

_____

Q & A WITH YOUR ANGEL

Enter your question for the angel in the spaces provided.

Q1. _____

_____

_____

Angel's Response (describe in detail what the angel has revealed to you and your interpretation of his message): _____

_____

_____

_____

_____

_____

Q2. _____

_____

_____

Angel's Response: _____

_____

_____

_____

_____

Q3. _____

_____

_____

Angel's Response: _____

_____

_____

_____

_____

Q4. _____

_____

_____

Angel's Response: _____

_____

_____

_____

_____

_____

Q5. _____

_____

_____

Angel's Response: _____

_____

_____

_____

_____

VALIDATION REQUEST

Ask your angel to validate this communication by sending some sort of sign. What sign does your angel say to watch for?

_____

_____

How are you feeling at the end of this exercise? Check all that apply and explain.

- ☐ Angry
- ☐ Anxious
- ☐ Assured
- ☐ Cheerful
- ☐ Connected (in the present)
- ☐ Depressed
- ☐ Detached (wandering thoughts)

- ☐ Eh, I'm all right, I guess
- ☐ Fearful
- ☐ Frustrated
- ☐ Happy
- ☐ Hesitant
- ☐ Lonely
- ☐ Motivated

- ☐ Peaceful
- ☐ Skeptical
- ☐ Tired/Weary
- ☐ Uncertain
- ☐ Warm and toasty inside
- ☐ Worry-worn

_____

_____

_____

_____

_____

_____

_____

VALIDATION UPDATE

Date your sign manifested: _____

How did your sign manifest? Was it different than you expected? _____

_____

_____

Describe the experience. Where were you? What were you doing? etc.

_____

_____

_____

_____

Additional Notes: _____

_____

_____

_____

_____

_____

4. Claircognizance

*(cognizance—knowing) The ability to suddenly know
information without prior reference or knowledge of how
the information was acquired.*

MERRIAM-WEBSTER'S DICTIONARY

Those of you blessed with claircognizance are said to have a direct connection to the legendary akashic records, the library of the cosmos. It is said that everything that's ever happened in the universe is recorded in this heavenly database, and some references go so far as to call it "the mind of God." I once thought, like many others, that the akashic records were a nineteenth-century myth, a story that somehow got attached to ancient Egypt. But when I encountered these records during a meditation tour with Archangel Gabriel, I was not only shocked that the library existed, but awed by its immeasurable size. The akashic records are a never-ending labyrinth of information—I saw towering walls, encrypted digital data streaming along them at warp speeds.

Very few people can access the akashic records—in fact, when I first saw them, Gabriel whisked me away so fast it made me dizzy. When I protested and asked to get a closer look, he simply said I wasn't ready yet to view the records. I eventually gained access to them several years later, but what's the use of having access to a library where all the contents are written in a language you can't read?

I expressed my frustration about this to Archangel Metatron, the keeper of the akashic records. He informed me that I need to read with my soul, not my physical eyes. Well, if that sounds abstract and obscure to you, you're not alone. I had absolutely no clue what he meant by that, because I was in fact in a meditation, with my eyes closed. I thought I *was* using my spiritual eyes! But the eyes he was talking about are the "eyes" of claircognizance—the eyes of knowing.

Claircognizance, however, is itself generated through a link to the akashic records. While I still attempt it from time to time, I know that since this gift relies on a library that few have access to, one cannot consciously "choose" claircognizance as a way of connecting with the angels. It's a skill that chooses you. Or rather, Metatron chooses you, since access to Heaven's mainframe is by invitation only.

In essence, those of you who have the gift most likely already know it, for you have the uncanny ability to know things without having to use normal channels. It's like pulling accurate information straight out of thin air. In actuality, you're connecting with Archangel Metatron, or his library assistant Archangel Ramiel, who allow you access to the most comprehensive database in all of Creation.

That being said, it won't hurt to test the waters and see if you have the gift. If you would like to experiment with claircognizance, see the exercise below. Before you start, look ahead to the pointers in chapter 4 about "Creating Your Sacred Space" (pg. 176) and "Grounding" (pg. 196). Also, you may want to photocopy this exercise for additional practice and keep your completed sheets in a binder.

ℛ Claircognizance Exercise
Knowledge from Your Angels

Today's Date _____

How are you feeling as you begin this exercise today? Check all that apply.

- ☐ Angry
- ☐ Anxious
- ☐ Assured
- ☐ Cheerful
- ☐ Connected
  (in the present)
- ☐ Depressed
- ☐ Detached
  (wandering thoughts)

- ☐ Eh, I'm all right,
  I guess
- ☐ Fearful
- ☐ Frustrated
- ☐ Happy
- ☐ Hesitant
- ☐ Lonely
- ☐ Motivated

- ☐ Peaceful
- ☐ Skeptical
- ☐ Tired/Weary
- ☐ Uncertain
- ☐ Warm and toasty
  inside
- ☐ Worry-worn

Making Contact

1. Prepare your sacred space, relax, and ground yourself. Make sure you are sitting in a comfortable position and breathe slowly.

2. Voice your intent for this exercise. **Example:** *My intent for this session is to connect with my parent/mentoring angel and to practice my intuitive skill of knowing.*

3. Close your eyes and concentrate on your breathing. Allow yourself to relax and shift your attention to the crown of your head. It is through the power channel of the crown chakra that you will connect with Heaven's database, otherwise known as the akashic records.

4. Ask Archangels Metatron and Ramiel to connect with you, so that you may receive their guidance through the labyrinth of this immeasurable library.

5. When you gain access, take a tour of the records with Heaven's resident librarians. Allow curiosity to be your friend and don't hesitate to ask questions. If there is something you aren't supposed to know, the angels will most assuredly inform you of that. Otherwise, enjoy the adventure and log your experience below. If, on the other hand, you can't seem to access the library, don't fret. Try other methods proposed in this workbook and try testing your claircognizance at a later time.

6. Upon leaving the library, don't forget to thank your host(s).

REVIEW YOUR EXPERIENCE

1. Who guided you through the library? _____

2. Describe your angel's presence.

   _____

   _____

3. How did your angel's presence make you feel? _____

   _____

4. Describe your visions, if any, of the library. Or describe any feelings or impressions you received about connecting with the akashic records.

   _____

   _____

   _____

   _____

5. Detail your discussion with your guides, and/or any information you gleaned while touring the library.

_____

_____

_____

_____

_____

_____

6. How will you be able to use this information in the human realm and apply it to your life or circumstances?

_____

_____

_____

_____

_____

Validation Request

Ask your angel to validate this communication by sending some sort of sign. What sign does your angel say to watch for?

_____

_____

How are you feeling at the end of this exercise? Check all that apply and explain.

- ☐ Angry
- ☐ Anxious
- ☐ Assured
- ☐ Cheerful
- ☐ Connected (in the present)
- ☐ Depressed
- ☐ Detached (wandering thoughts)

- ☐ Eh, I'm all right, I guess
- ☐ Fearful
- ☐ Frustrated
- ☐ Happy
- ☐ Hesitant
- ☐ Lonely
- ☐ Motivated

- ☐ Peaceful
- ☐ Skeptical
- ☐ Tired/Weary
- ☐ Uncertain
- ☐ Warm and toasty inside
- ☐ Worry-worn

_____

_____

_____

_____

_____

_____

VALIDATION UPDATE

Date your sign manifested: _____

How did your sign manifest? Was it different than you expected? _____

_____

_____

Describe the experience. Where were you? What were you doing? etc.

_____

_____

_____

_____

Additional Notes: _____

_____

_____

_____

_____

_____

5. *Intuition*

1: quick and ready insight 2a: immediate apprehension or cognition b: knowledge or conviction gained by intuition c: the power or faculty of attaining to direct knowledge or cognition without evident rational thought and inference.

MERRIAM-WEBSTER'S DICTIONARY

Based on the above definition, intuition sounds a lot like claircognizance. But I consider it to be slightly different, in that intuition involves a combination of some (or all) of the extrasensory perception skills I discuss above. Instead of being confined to one distinct skill, intuition is a subtle amalgamation of clairaudience, clairsentience, clairvoyance, and claircognizance. While one person may have a full conversation with her angels during meditation, or another may have clear visions of his guides, a person relying on old-fashioned intuition receives her messages much more subtly. When working with your intuition, you may hear the slightest of whispers or have a premonition, but for you, this is more than enough information.

If your inclination is intuitive, then you probably already know to go with the first thought that comes to mind when seeking messages from the Divine. Still, don't fall into the trap of overanalyzing how you got the information, or the information itself.

I tell all my students and clients that everyone is intuitive in some capacity. Everyone. It's the feeling a mother gets when her child is in danger. Or the chill that runs up your spine when you encounter a stranger with ill intentions. It's that inner voice telling you everything is going to work out just fine, even as you sit in the midst of a crisis.

If you would like to experiment with intuition, see the exercise below, which is formatted as a log. The Intuition Log is simply a journal where you can keep track of your daily "hits"—your accurate perceptions or predictions—as you consciously and actively engage your intuition. There is no preparation for this. You are simply recording your spiritual experiences in the field, as it were.

For example, when you get an inkling about something at work, something in your relationship, or something in the world around you, jot it down in your log and wait for things to manifest. You could have an intuition about something as simple as knowing who is on the phone before looking at the caller ID, or thinking of a friend you haven't talked to in a long while, only to hear from them out of the blue. Or you could discover, after the fact, that your unease about stepping into a business partnership was on point and helped you avoid a financial upset.

Keeping track of these types of experiences will help you become more aware of your intuitive abilities and how to fine-tune them. You may even discover that you have new strengths or abilities, related to the other methods of connecting, that you weren't previously aware of.

As you chronicle your intuitive moments, don't be discouraged if you have more misses than hits. In other words, don't consider it a failure if a gut feeling or a sudden thought does not manifest in any sort of outcome. Remember, this is about *practicing* the art of intuition. Learning about the cues that your body and your physical and spiritual environments send to you will help you better understand how to develop this skill. You may want to photocopy the log for additional practice and keep your completed sheets in a binder.

❧ INTUITION LOG
Angel Whispers

Today's Date _____

How are you feeling today? Check all that apply.

- ☐ Angry
- ☐ Anxious
- ☐ Assured
- ☐ Cheerful
- ☐ Connected
  (in the present)
- ☐ Depressed
- ☐ Detached
  (wandering thoughts)

- ☐ Eh, I'm all right,
  I guess
- ☐ Fearful
- ☐ Frustrated
- ☐ Happy
- ☐ Hesitant
- ☐ Lonely
- ☐ Motivated

- ☐ Peaceful
- ☐ Skeptical
- ☐ Tired/Weary
- ☐ Uncertain
- ☐ Warm and toasty
  inside
- ☐ Worry-worn

What were the circumstances surrounding your intuitive insight?

_____

_____

_____

_____

_____

_____

_____

_____

How did your intuition figure into the experience? What information did it provide?

_____

_____

_____

_____

_____

Did you have a specific query in mind at the time you engaged your intuition? (should I go to the office party or skip out, take the long way home instead of the freeway, etc.) If so, write it here:

_____

_____

_____

Did you experience an extraordinary outcome as a result of following your intuition? (I got the chance to meet an influential executive, avoided a multicar pileup, etc.) If so, write it here:

_____

_____

_____

What would you consider this intuitive experience?   Hit   Miss

If you encountered a miss, what do you think hampered you? (emotions, desired results, etc.)

_____

_____

_____

Additional Notes: _____

_____

_____

_____

_____

_____

_____

_____

_____

_____

6. Dreams

Archangels Raphael and Cassiel love weaving in and out of dreamscape, but that does not mean that you dreamers out there won't ever catch a glimpse of Iophiel's latest fashions or hear Sandalphon's latest symphony. Because our human minds are most impressionable when we're asleep, the angels can and often do use dreams as a vehicle for delivering their messages.

If you look at the many stories found throughout the world's religions, you will find that someone is always dreaming. From the ancient Babylonian king Nebuchad-nezzar in the *Book of Daniel* to Queen Maya, mother of Gautama Buddha, dreamers have always painted our religious and spiritual landscapes. Why should we be so foolish as to believe that in the modern age, dreams are no longer a viable way to connect with the Divine?

However, unlike in the days of old, we don't exactly have a court of prophets we can run to that can decipher our dreams for us. Sure, there are dream interpreters out there, but I promise you that if you go to ten different interpreters, you're going to get ten different interpretations. The same can be said for dream interpretation books. Interpreters and books both claim to have an understanding of how dreams work, but as I mentioned in the discussion of clairvoyance, no one can tell you what a rose means for *you*. You have to decipher that for yourself. Yes, we all can tell you what symbols commonly mean, but it's purely subjective. If you ask a Funda-mentalist Christian what a dragon represents, she will more than likely say that it represents Satan. If you ask someone from China, he'll likely tell you that a dragon foretells great fortune.

The same goes for colors and numbers. White represents purity in the West, but it represents death in the East. The number five in Western numerology is a "bad luck" number to be avoided, while in the East it's one of the most fortunate of all numbers.

You could also go to someone who specializes in dream therapy. At that point, however, your dreams are going to be interpreted through the filters of psychother-apy, by a person who will most likely think you should be committed if you tell them you're trying to connect with your angels.

So, where does this leave you? It leaves you with the one thing you'll ever need: yourself. Trust your own natural intuitive skills when deciphering what your dream means. While I'm in no way telling you to avoid interpreters or books, I'm saying that to rely solely upon them defeats the purpose of getting to know and understand your angels and guides *on your own terms*.

And to be perfectly fair, the same goes when it comes to this book. My purpose in being an author and angel medium is not to keep you coming back to me every time you encounter a life crisis. Not to sound harsh or cruel, but my task is not to hold my client's hand. Rather, it's to guide them to their angels, who will do the hand-holding. I'm merely a telephone operator who can help you connect to your angels, but once you figure out how to dial them up yourself, my job is done. There are plenty of clients and students who can attest to this—I've no hesitation whatsoever to tell someone they don't need a consultation. And if the angels shake their heads *no*, that means my clients and students need to figure out a particular issue for themselves, anyhow. It may take a long time to fully understand some of your dreams, but that just might be the challenge the angels have set for you.

One dream that took me years to understand occurred when I was just beginning college. I dreamt that I was standing in my driveway looking up into a starry night sky. Suddenly, all these ghostly blue faces appeared. Their lips were moving as if they were talking to me, but I couldn't hear a word. I remember being more awed than afraid, but I quickly grew frustrated since I desperately wanted to know what the faces were saying. Perturbed, I growled and stamped my foot. Big mistake. A chill went up my spine, and I looked up at the second-story balcony of my neighbor's house. A large black dragon was perched there. His gaze narrowed on me and he let out a roar that shook the ground beneath my feet. He then belched a stream of flames in my direction, and I instantly awoke.

The dream didn't frighten me, but it left me vexed and wondering what it meant. Roughly five years later, when I began encountering one archangel after another, I figured out what that dream had portended. The archangels, I believe, were represented by the faces peering down at me from Heaven.

I also eventually encountered the dragon. His name is Black, and he is one of Archangel Uriel's pet dragons. This dark and brooding beast is a lot like Uriel, who doesn't stand for nonsense or insolence. Black's reprimand, that night in my dream, was meant as a warning for me to tread lightly, yet dutifully, while under the direct tutelage of the angels. Unfortunately, it was a warning that I didn't bother to heed when I first met the angels, and I wound up getting singed on many occasions. But you live and learn and lick your wounds, while pondering the missteps you won't be making again anytime soon.

Given the time it sometimes takes to fully grasp the meaning of dreams, this method of connecting with the angels can be a bit slower than clairaudience or clairvoyance. Don't despair, however, for you will receive your message and its meaning exactly when you're supposed to. So, don't mull over possible interpretations of your dreams for too long, since it may be years before your dream makes sense.

I know that some of you may already be cringing at the notion of using dreams to connect, because dreams can be difficult to remember. Remembering takes a lot of practice, and one of the best ways to practice is journaling. To that end I've provided a Dreams Log, below.

Regardless of how you approach your dreams and this log, please be sure to do so with an open heart and mind. Some of you may dream in black and white. Others may dream in Technicolor, with surround sound and smell-o-vision. But no matter how you dream, do your best to get the most out of it by keeping track of your sleepy-time visions as best you can. It helps to write your dream down as soon as you think of it—otherwise, it can evaporate. If you're looking to use dreams as a primary method of connecting, assiduous practice in remembering them is of the essence.

Working with dreams can be a challenging task. Based on my personal experience, along with what clients and students have told me, it's a bit difficult to get answers to questions you've asked before going sleep. Of course, this is not the case for everyone—I've had a handful of clients express joy that Raphael came to them in a dream just as they'd asked.

But not all of us are going to be that successful.

You'll notice that the Dreams Log does not require you to ask questions before entering the dreamscape. You can if you wish, but I believe that when it comes to dreams, it may be prudent to let the angels have control of the messages they deliver. After all, they know best, and this approach will help us avoid feeling disappointed if we don't get exactly what we ask for.

While trying to connect with your angels this way, some of you may even get the pleasure of experiencing lucid dreams—dreams in which you are fully aware that you're dreaming. If there was ever a time to take advantage of dreams, this is it. So, if in a dream you suddenly realize that you're dreaming, don't hesitate to call upon your angels and guides. Some of the best visitations I've experienced were during lucid dreaming sessions when I had enough wits about me to call on my spirit guide. Within a heartbeat, he appeared, ready to talk.

Along these lines, I've found that the mere appearance of angels during a dream can often jar you into the lucid state. Their presence can turn an ordinary dream into one in which you are self-aware and in control of your visions. In this lucid dream state, you are able to better engage your angels and guides—your critical mind is accessible, now, and you'll be more likely to ask them questions, as well as remember the answers when you wake.

I encourage you to make additional copies of the Dreams Log, to keep in a binder. Remember to read back through your log every now and then to see if the meaning of any of your dreams has manifested.

❧ DREAMS LOG
Angel Vistas

Today's Date _____

Before you went to bed, how did you feel? Check all that apply.

- ☐ Angry
- ☐ Anxious
- ☐ Assured
- ☐ Cheerful
- ☐ Connected
  (in the present)
- ☐ Depressed
- ☐ Detached
  (wandering thoughts)

- ☐ Eh, I'm all right,
  I guess
- ☐ Fearful
- ☐ Frustrated
- ☐ Happy
- ☐ Hesitant
- ☐ Lonely
- ☐ Motivated

- ☐ Peaceful
- ☐ Skeptical
- ☐ Tired/Weary
- ☐ Uncertain
- ☐ Warm and toasty
  inside
- ☐ Worry-worn

When you went to bed...

☐ You fell asleep as soon as your head hit the pillow.

☐ You watched a little television. What did you watch?

_____

☐ You did some reading. What did you read?

_____

☐ You talked with your bedmate. Care to elaborate?

_____

_____

_____

☐ You stared at the ceiling/tossed and turned.

☐ Other. Please specify.

_____

_____

_____

_____

Did you ask your angels to connect with you in your dreams?

☐ No

☐ Yes

Did you request to see a specific angel? Yes No

If yes, who? _____

If you asked them to address a certain issue, write it here.

_____

_____

_____

Describe the dream, if any, that led up to your meeting with your angel.

_____

_____

_____

Which angel/guide appeared to you in your dream? _____

How did you know who it was? (he told you, wrote his name in the clouds, you just knew, etc.)

_____

_____

What gender did your angel appear to be?   Male   Female

Describe your angel's appearance in as much detail as possible (clothing, build, etc.).

_____

_____

_____

Describe any icons your angel may have been holding when he appeared (shield, crystal, flowers, etc.).

_____

_____

How did your angel's appearance make you feel? (serene, concerned, curious, etc.)

_____

_____

Describe here what transpired, if anything, between you and your angel during this encounter.

_____

_____

_____

Describe here what transpired, if anything, after you and your angel parted.

_____

_____

_____

Was this a lucid dream?   Yes   No

    If yes, how/when did you become self-aware in your dream?

_____

_____

When did you first remember your dream?

    ☐ The moment you awoke.

    ☐ A few minutes later.

    ☐ A few hours later.

    ☐ Other _____

How did you feel when you first awoke?

_____

_____

How did you feel when you first remembered your dream? (if different)

_____

_____

What do you think this dream could mean for you, if anything?

_____

_____

_____

_____

If you are consulting dream interpretation books, list their interpretations here.

_____

_____

_____

_____

_____

Validation Sign

Did your angel tell you of a sign that would be validation of this communication? If you don't remember one, don't fret. Write down the most significant things you remember about your dream—are there other signs you could watch for?

_____

_____

_____

_____

Validation Update 1

Date your sign manifested: _____

How did your sign manifest? Was it different than you expected? _____

_____

_____

Type of validation:

☐ Angelic validation (the manifestation of a sign your angel instructed you to look for).

☐ Dream validation (the manifestation of a sign that appeared vividly in your dream).

☐ Personal validation (the manifestation of a sign that appears to support your original dream interpretation).

☐ Book validation (the manifestation of a sign that correlates directly with an angelic icon listed in this book or with a dream interpretation from another dream book). Write the book title here.

_____

Describe your experience. When your sign appeared, where were you? What were you doing? etc.

_____

_____

_____

Additional Notes:

_____

_____

_____

VALIDATION UPDATE 2 (IF APPLICABLE)

Date your sign manifested: _____

How did your sign manifest? Was it different than you expected? _____

_____

_____

Type of validation:

- ☐ Angelic validation (the manifestation of a sign your angel instructed you to look for).

- ☐ Dream validation (the manifestation of a sign that appeared vividly in your dream).

- ☐ Personal validation (the manifestation of a sign that appears to support your original dream interpretation).

- ☐ Book validation (the manifestation of a sign that correlates directly to an angelic icon listed in this book or with a dream interpretation from another dream book). Write the book title here.

_____

Describe your experience. When your sign appeared, where were you? What were you doing? etc.

_____

_____

_____

Additional Notes:

_____

_____

_____

7. Signs

By now, you've most likely figured out that I'm a skeptic and a cynic when it comes to all things spiritual and religious. Having endured painful disillusionment brought about by institutions of church and education, it's very difficult for me to simply follow along blindly. Even when Jesus began talking to me, I didn't believe it and sought to explain it away as a momentary lapse of sanity. But what finally made me stop and take notice were the many strange and mysterious things that were occurring in my life—in other words, the manifestations of signs that validated much of what the voices in my head were saying.

A good test for all of us who are journeying down a spiritual path is to seek out signs confirming that our communication with the realm of spirit is real, not a mere play upon the psyche. Since the archangels, as well as JC, are well aware of my Doubting Thomas nature, they are merciful enough to humor me in my disbelief. Though I've desperately tried to tamp down my skepticism, it still often gets the best of me. Whenever the angels have a message for me, I tend to cross my arms over my chest and say, "I'll believe it when I see it."

I admit, this stubbornness is getting old. After all, you would think that after my stroke I would be more malleable. And in many ways, I am. Instead of fighting the angels and going left when they instruct me to go right, I now simply acquiesce with a grumble or two and go along with the program. It's much easier for me this way.

Since the release of *Azrael Loves Chocolate*, I have gotten a slew of emails asking how I can be so skeptical of the angels when they have clearly proven their presence in my life. The answer to that is easy: I never expect the past to predicate the future. This is a turbulent spiritual road to travel, to be sure, but the moment I start believing things blindly is the moment I need to stop what I'm doing as an angel medium. With this gift comes great responsibility, so what you may see as doubt or faithlessness on my part is merely my way of keeping myself in check. After all, my doubt is not in God or his messengers, but in my own humanness.

And of course, it's only natural to believe what we can witness with our five senses, right? Well, sometimes we refuse to even believe those!

For example, the Bible tells the story of how Egypt was plagued by the wrath of God before Pharaoh allowed the Jewish slaves to leave the kingdom. When the Jews were released, they found themselves trapped between the Red Sea and the pharaoh's armies. Despite what they had seen transpire in Egypt, they feared for their lives. Then God parted the sea, allowing them to pass while drowning their pursuers.

The Jews wandered the desert for what seemed like an eternity but never hungered, for God allowed manna to rain from the heavens to feed them. Even then, they still doubted that Moses would return to them from Mount Sinai, where he'd gone to receive God's instruction, and they were quick to turn their worship toward a golden calf.

See a pattern here?

If you read through Exodus, you'll see that God gave the Jews one miraculous sign after another, and still people doubted. We all have our moments of doubt—even JC had his moment of doubt at his crucifixion (do you blame him?). But when I catch myself doubting an angelic message, I shake my head in shame and say, "I may have my doubts, but I'm not gonna build a golden calf…yet."

Of course, in this day and age we don't get to witness the parting of great seas or feel grain rain down from Heaven. Most miracles today are a little subtler, to the point where many of us, myself included, are quick to call them coincidences. May we bite our tongues! I always ask for signs, not just for myself but for all of my clients, students, and readers who are beginning to establish connections with their angels. Seeing such signs pulls us up out of blind faith and elevates us to a more resilient faith—one backed by the understanding that God is in control. I don't base my faith on the fact that God previously bailed me out of a tight situation, but on the fact that God is guiding my every step.

Everyone can say they talk to God. Everyone can say that God talks back to them. I won't argue that one bit, but I personally find it comforting to have validation that it's truly God I'm communicating with, not the voice of my own desires and agendas. That said, expect to encounter quite a few surprises as you embark upon your spiritual endeavor. You may find that some of the things you've learned in life up to this point aren't as they seem. They may be misconstrued, outmoded, or outright false. Not to minimize the issue, but it's like Yoda once told Luke Skywalker: "You must unlearn all that you have learned."

When you go through life believing one way, and then the Creator and his messengers come to you and say, "Well, it's not *exactly* that way, it's more like…", they don't expect you to simply take their words at face value. Or, depending on who you are, maybe they do, but I have always tested and retested these messengers before accepting what they had to teach.

I can only implore that you do the same, especially in the beginning. Regardless of the method you use to connect with your angels and guides, don't hesitate to ask for signs as validation. Write down what the angels communicate to you, and then wait for the signs to manifest.

For those of you just starting out, however, working with signs can be frustrating as well as exciting. I always like to use the "dove" analogy when explaining this: If you're connecting with Archangel Raphael and you ask for a sign, he may whisper or show you a white dove. This doesn't mean that you should run outside to search the skies all day. Doing so would distract you from the convoy of Dove ice cream trucks rolling by.

You may wonder why the archangel didn't just simply instruct you to look for ice cream trucks. For some of you, he may very well have been that specific, but for those of you just learning how to train your senses to recognize an angelic presence in your life, the word "dove" is all you really need. Besides, "ice cream" isn't really Raphael's style. Archangel Sandalphon, who loves sweets, would most likely say "ice cream." Warrior Archangel Michael might use "convoy." But from the wise and gentle Raphael, you would hear the word "dove."

A client once shared with me her experience with clairaudience, and we were joking about the Dove ice cream truck analogy. Her take on it was that we humans simply hear what we want to hear. Raphael may have said "Dove ice cream truck," but the only thing that got through all the human filters and walls we've spent a lifetime building was the word "dove." In this way, connecting with the angels can be a lot like trying to talk to your friend on a cell phone…while driving through a tunnel. The difference between the angels and your friend on the phone, however, is that the angels know which words you're going to pick up, hence taking the randomness out of the message they're sending—whereas your friend has absolutely no idea what you're picking up, in between the static and the intermittent silence.

Another interesting thing about looking for signs is that they never turn up in the place where you expect them to. For example, I was experiencing a tense situation with a colleague, and there was a lot of stress between us. Metatron happened to be the angel "on call" that day. Or rather, he was the one who answered when I looked heavenward with tearful eyes, pleading for help. He assured me that everything would work out, but I was so distraught over the situation that I didn't want a pep talk—I just wanted him to do something. (Remember, angels don't fix anything; they merely help us to go through the challenges we're supposed to face in life.) I could feel him smiling down upon me as he reassured me again, and like the curmudgeon I was that day, I replied, "Yeah, sure. This situation is *fubared*. Nothing is going to fix it at this point."

"You will find a resolution," he offered lovingly.

"Oh? Could you give me a little sign, then? I just really need to know that this too shall pass."

"Look for elephants."

Elephants. *Elephants!* Was the archangel kidding? I scoffed at this supposed sign, but all morning I hoped I'd come across a picture of elephants on the Internet or something. As the day progressed, I completely forgot about elephants and headed out to a doctor appointment. As I crossed the hospital lobby, I suddenly remembered that I needed to buy stamps, so I hightailed it to the gift shop. And there, in the gift shop window, was a family of elephant statues. There wasn't one or two, but at least a half dozen. And these statues weren't small, either. They were floor statues, made of carved wood, with a huge sign in front of them that read *New Arrivals*. Stupefied, I stood there gazing at the carvings.

At that point, I could only throw my hands up in surrender.

"You got me," I whispered heavenward. Needless to say, the situation with my colleague smoothed right out, just like Metatron had said it would.

But not everything is so black and white when it comes to deciphering signs. That's evident in the emails and phone calls I receive from clients and students who get a sign from their angel and then don't know what to do with it.

Too many times the conversation goes something like this:

> CLIENT: Michael showed me red balloons in my meditation, and when I got to work today all of our cubicles had red balloons tied to them. So, what is Michael telling me?

Chantel: Well, it's definitely a sign that he's with you and connecting with you, but did you ask him anything?

Client: I really want to put my name in the hat for a promotion, but I'm not sure if I want to put up with the management games. I asked him to give me a sign and he showed me red balloons.

Chantel: Okay, I hear you, but what did you ask him?

Do you see where the problem is here? This actually happens quite often. Someone will get excited that their angel gave them a sign that manifested, but the sign is confusing because the person didn't *specifically* ask for anything. For our sake, not the angels', our questions must be as concise as possible. Don't ask questions like, "Should I or shouldn't I go for that job promotion?" Simply ask, "Should I?"

In some ways, this seems to be falling into the trap of fortune-telling. While I too have found myself pining to know the future, we have to practice restraint, because the decisions that we're asking for help with have already been made. Before she was born, my client had already made the decision whether or not to go for the promotion. Her asking Michael if she should or shouldn't is completely irrelevant, for she's locked into her destiny just like the rest of us. Regardless of how the archangel answers her or the signs he gives, her soul already made the decision years ago, when she was scripting her life to be included in God's Great Equation.

Let me give you an example of how the conversation with Michael would go if it had been me in my client's shoes:

Chantel: Mike, I really want that job promotion. It means more money, a bit more creative freedom, and I wouldn't have to answer to my supervisor anymore.

Archangel Michael: True, but it also means you're going to be salaried and you'll be working some weekends. You're already a workaholic. Do you really want the added stress?

Chantel: (*Whimper.*) But if I stay in this position, there's no telling when another promotion will come my way.

Archangel Michael: Chantel, you already know the answer to this one.

Chantel: I know. I just like talking it out with you.

Archangel Michael: You can't make a wrong decision. Whichever route you take will bring with it lessons to be learned.

Chantel: Some easier than others.

Archangel Michael: No, not necessarily. You're going to complain either way.

And he's right about that. After a few cleansing breaths, I would decide to go for the promotion. The next day, however, I'd most likely chicken out. But that was supposed to happen. The promotion wasn't meant to be, which then raises the question of what staying in my current position could mean.

Only time will tell, and eventually, the whys will make themselves known. At that point, you can begin to understand the reasons why you made the decision you did. Life is never about making decisions, but about learning from them.

The purpose of every decision we make is to teach us lessons. For my client, it was never about applying for the promotion or not, but gaining wisdom from whichever path she chose. And so it is for you, me, and everyone else in this world. Because of this, I ask that you look for signs casually, with an open mind, and not become obsessed with trying to find them and dissect what they mean. At the very foundation, they really only mean one thing—that your angels are walking beside you every step of the way as you journey through life.

I would be remiss at this point not to include a note about "Not Signs." Many of you may have seen things (orbs, shadows, floating and twinkling lights, bodies of fog, apparitions) that you may be tempted to take as "evidence" of angelic presence. I receive many inquiries regarding such sightings. While this may come as a surprise to you, given my enthusiasm for validating angelic presence through signs, I must also ask that you exercise caution when encountering phenomena such as those described above. Because we are so desperate for contact with the angels, we often rush to believe that unexplained occurrences or sights indicate an angelic presence. I think that this belief is naïve at best and reckless at worst—the human eye is very easy to trick, and susceptible to external elements such as lighting and movement that can contribute to "seeing" something that may or may not be present.

Because such occurrences can cause a lot of excitement and heightened emotion, make sure you're grounded before you form any conclusions about what you saw. Once you've taken a few breaths, tap into your spiritual self. Ask yourself how the sighting made you feel. Did you truly feel an otherworldly presence? If so, did it feel calm, loving, comforting, and peaceful? Truly search your feelings and try to remain objective.

While the angels love to have fun just like we do, they're not in the business of wowing us with sideshow antics such as roaming shadows or furniture that skids across the room. So let's not get too caught up in Hollywood theatrics. The angels tend to have a much more subtle approach. If they want to connect with you, they can clue you in without causing chaos.

Another way to discern whether unexplained phenomena somehow indicates an angelic presence is the question of consistency. Michael, for example, will give off small flashes of light to let you know he's around, but he will also let you know he's there by using connections that you've already established with him, be it clairaudience, dreams, etc. It is much better to foster this kind of relationship with your angels, seeking out connection through personal, intimate experiences every day, rather than relying on spectacle.

Spirituality is personal. I can't emphasize this enough. Get to know God, the angels, Jesus, Mary, Buddha, Ganesh, and so on for yourself. It's not about rites and rituals. It's not about pomp and ceremony. And it's certainly not about spectacles like apparitions and séances, most of which, I believe, are contrived merely for the sake of entertainment.

Because I am unwavering in this belief, I keep my Angel Gallery events limited to a very small number of people (usually a dozen or fewer), and I prefer to conduct consultations in private settings as opposed to reading for large audiences. The connections that we establish with the Divine are something to be cherished, and approached as opportunities for reflection and self-discovery, *not* entertainment. This isn't to say that the angels aren't a fun bunch to hang out with—they are. But they make their company enjoyable so that humans are more accepting of them and more receptive to their messages. They're not trying to boost ratings on some cable channel broadcasting from Heaven.

To begin deciphering and understanding how signs manifest in your Angel Code, please turn to page 245 and complete a Life Log. You will have the opportunity to record the validation signs you receive. Let your own experiences with the angels renew and fortify your faith in them … and in yourself.

8. *Other Methods of Connecting*

And speaking of entertainment, I'll complete this chapter by discussing a few popular methods of connecting that clients have asked me about, over the years, in their quests to make contact with the realm of spirit. These methods include, but are certainly not limited to, things of an occult nature such as pendulums, crystal balls, mirror or water scrying, tea leaf reading, automatic writing, table tipping, planchettes (Ouija boards), and the always popular tarot cards.

My thoughts on these methods? Basically, I think that many of them are a crutch; once you tap into your own natural intuitive skills, you'll quickly realize that you don't need any of this stuff. Methods such as the planchettes and table tipping I have other reservations about (although for different reasons than you might expect).

But first, let's talk tarot. To be perfectly honest, I admit that I used tarot cards during much of my youth (often while listening to Led Zeppelin's "Kashmir"). At the time, I was seeking to predict the future, not establish any contact with the realm of spirit. Once I became a born-again Christian, of course, the cards went into the garbage can. But when I left the church years later, my curiosity led me right back to them.

It wasn't until I met my spiritual mentor a few years after that, however, that I discovered tarot cards based on angels. For the longest time, I had been using a set that I'd created myself, but when I first discovered the different types of angel cards sold in the bookstores, I immediately took to them. Fortunately, I quickly discovered that the power was not in the cards, but in me.

Let me tell you a story about that...

One Sunday afternoon, I stopped by to visit my mentor, Ella. Being her usual cheery self, she announced, "In a few weeks we're having Angels Day here at the tea shop. Another store in the complex is sponsoring it, but I thought it'd be nice if we participated, too."

"Angels?" *Ugh*, I thought. Even as much as I loved Ella and felt grateful for her guidance in my life, I couldn't say I was all that excited about the news.

"Yeah, we're going to have readers up here that weekend." She beamed.

"Cool!" Okay, now I was interested. "I'll come up and get a reading."

Ella's eyes leveled sternly upon me. "No, you don't get it, kiddo. You're one of my readers."

All right, Ella was pretty much my adopted mother by this point. And I had quickly learned that you just did not tell this determined sage "no." So I swallowed hard, forced a smile, and politely informed her that I hadn't really worked with my tarot cards in nearly two years.

"Well, Angels Day is in two weeks. I suggest you get practicing." By her tone, I knew the conversation was over. In any discussion, Ella was almost always the ruling majority. Pouting, I agreed just to hear myself agree, and left to go and consider her request. As I wandered through the stores adjacent to her shop, I finally stumbled into a little gift store specializing in angel figurines. Obviously, I had found the store sponsoring Angels Day. I gave a quick glance of spite heavenward and walked grudgingly inside.

I browsed the shop with a sour face, fighting with my inability to believe in these winged creatures. I couldn't help but think that a spirit guide had more time to help me out than an archangel did.

I would soon discover that this notion was completely wrong.

As I meandered through the aisles and past tables upon tables of angel trinkets and figurines, I came to a card display and picked up a deck of popular angel divination cards. My jaw hit the floor. I had no idea angel cards existed. I curiously flipped through the display, finding them alluring and their energy inviting. So, naturally, I introduced myself to the store's owner as one of Ella's readers, bought the cards, and took them home to practice.

Two weeks passed, and I found myself waking up that brisk January morning with a sense of defeat. My new deck of angel cards sat on the nightstand, barely touched, since my eagerness to use them had waned about a week after purchasing them. It wasn't the cards, though; I just didn't want to be a reader.

With a growl, I sat up and stared at the clock. I drew my hands over my face and looked to the ceiling, hoping God would tell me I didn't have to go if I really didn't want to. I honestly wanted to call Ella and tell her I couldn't make it. Yep, I was planning on calling in sick, but then felt a twinge of pain in my rear end and heard Ella's subtle but stern voice in my head.

Get your butt up here.

"All right, I'm coming!" I glared at the ceiling. Ella was always an early bird, and she had sent her message to my telepathic inbox so that it was there and waiting when I awoke. With much trepidation, I drove forty minutes north to the teashop where Ella, as expected, greeted me with a smile and a tight hug.

"You get my message?" Her eyes were bright with amusement. Once you enter the company of someone as powerful as Ella, things such as telepathy and precognizance become the norm. In the years I'd known her, I'd come to expect them of her, so I simply growled back in response to her gloating.

"I can't do this. I haven't read for many paying customers before. What if I'm wrong?" I was shaking as I followed Ella around the store. When we entered the room where I was to give the readings, she took me by the shoulders and looked me in the eyes.

"The day you learn to surrender, Chantel, is the day the entire universe will open up for you. You're like a frightened little girl who keeps testing the waters, as if they'll get warmer each time you test. Well, news flash for you, kiddo: you're just going to have to take the plunge and let your soul acclimate to whatever God has in store for you." She said those words so sincerely and lovingly that I found myself holding my breath while listening to her.

"Surrender." She shook my shoulders. "Surrender and you'll be just fine."

"But what if…" I was still trembling, just terrified of disappointing her and her customers.

"There is no *what if*." She headed out of the room. "We're booked solid today. Your first client arrives in about ten minutes."

Nervous, I sat down in my chair and pulled out my cards and cute gypsy props such as candles and crystals. None of which had any meaning at the time. I had read for a few paying customers before, but nothing near the scale of what Ella would bring in that day.

In exactly ten minutes, my first customer stuck her head in my room to see if I was ready. I sat there with a smile plastered on my face and a bit of sweat on my brow. I offered her a seat and had her shuffle the deck of angel cards. While she shuffled, I jotted down the word "surrender" on the back of a business card and propped it up so I could glance at it every now and then. By that time, the client handed the deck of angel cards back to me and, with a smile, I began to place them one by one on the table.

I looked at the cards for about two minutes, and quickly came to the conclusion that I had absolutely no idea what the spread meant.

After about two seconds of panic, I took a deep breath and reshuffled the deck. I tried not to acknowledge the confused expression on my client's face and laid the cards out again. Still they made no sense. It was then that I glanced at the business card with the word "surrender" scrawled on it. I closed my eyes.

Within seconds I saw a beautiful, angelic face. It smiled warmly at me, and then the image zoomed out a bit to reveal a young woman with soft brown hair and even softer eyes. She gazed at me a moment and my fear disappeared completely.

Mother Mary? I spoke to her in my mind. Her eyes twinkled as she adjusted her veil, which was aglow with golden light.

Why are you here? I'm not Catholic! I tensed.

No, but she is. The Virgin Mother pointed to my client. *I am not concerned with what religion you believe in, child. I've a message for her and you will be my voice.* The beautiful Queen of Angels spoke some more, and I relayed the message as fluidly as it came to me.

After the message was delivered, I saw a swirl of colors, and it only took me a few seconds to realize that I was seeing my client's aura and chakras. I could see a haze in her heart chakra, and her root chakra looked like raw ground beef. I relayed this information to the client, and then realized that I had to quickly translate what I saw into laymen's terms. I warned her of breathing problems, and that it seemed she was either getting over them or starting them. I also noted a brick wall around her heart and then the shielding of what was left of her shredded root chakra. After thirty straight minutes of talking, the images began to fade and I was left sitting there thinking, *this woman is going to ask for a refund.*

When I opened my eyes, the woman's jaw was on the table and she had been weeping. She told me that she'd just finalized her divorce, was getting over a bad bout of bronchitis, and was fighting irritable bowel syndrome as well. We then began discussing a philosophy that the acclaimed medical intuitive Dr. Caroline Myss has coined: "Your biography is your biology." We talked about how the stress of a poor marriage had taken its toll on her physical health, and spiritual exercises that she could use to help alleviate that stress. That's when I recommended a few books on meditation and spiritual healing and sent her on her way.

I sat in the room a minute in silence, just staring at the business card and the word "surrender." But what had happened didn't really dawn on me yet. I just thought it was beginner's luck, and that the first client was a fluke. Well, if that was the case, I had nine more flukes that day.

At the end of Angels Day, I was still oblivious to what had happened, but admitted to Ella that the day wasn't as bad as I had anticipated. She simply smiled, patted me on the back, and bid me a good night. I know she wanted to say, "I told you so," but Ella had what I'd like to think of as an elevated spirit. Well, that, and the fact that she also had four children, and most likely knew that such gloating would be met with rebellion, a tantrum, or both.

On the way home, I tried my best to process the day and what it meant to me, but I found myself slipping into doubt as easily as I would an old pair of comfortable jeans. The rest of my night was spent mulling over all the readings I had done, trying desperately to debunk them. What I couldn't chalk up to merely luck or coincidence, I tried to blame on the clients and their "naive willingness" to just piece together the information I gave them to suit their needs.

My analyses were like those of the skeptics and critics who are eager to debunk psychics, and I was playing both sides of the fence only to arrive at an impasse. In one breath, I was simultaneously awed and scared by the gift that had been given to me. In the next, I felt that I had skipped by on sheer dumb luck. In the following breath, I contemplated how much further I could take my gift, connecting with even more people. In the next breath, I felt like a fake, a phony, a fraud. Would I be one hundred percent accurate all the time, or just a tenth of the time? Would I be appreciated for my gifts, or burned at the stake? Would I be known as an oracle, or a heretic?

So many thoughts went through my mind as I tried to fall asleep that evening. I simply didn't know what to make of the fact that out of ten readings, ten people left with answers and information they could weave seamlessly into the intricate tapestries of their lives, all of it validated by references I had absolutely no way of knowing beforehand.

While this story illustrates my tendency to not believe my own eyes (and in this case, the successful readings), it also shows how my prop—the angel cards—were not really the source of my insights into my clients' lives. As months passed, I got to the point where using cards seemed laughable. Then Ella told me something that stunned me, and still stuns me even unto this day. She said that intuitives walk a fine line between spirituality and business, and that whether I actually used the cards or not was irrelevant. Since people who go to psychics often want to see cards laid out on a table and have their fortunes told, doing so can be a good business decision. But like a magician's magic top hat, the cards are just props—merely there for show.

And so it is in your life, as well. The power is within you, not within whatever prop you may be using.

The issue of fortune-telling is something I war with more than anything. How can people be so obsessed with career, finance, love, and family when the messengers of God are looking over their shoulders? I once had a client who had not one, not two, but a *choir* of angels standing behind her, and all she could do was complain that her daughter was making the wrong choice about the man she was about to marry.

Is this painful to endure? You bet it was. For years I had to begin each consultation with a preamble: "I'm not a fortune-teller, more like a telephone operator that helps you to connect to your angels and guides." Still, no matter how often I say that, people only want one thing, really—for the angels to fix their lives for them in the course of forty-five minutes.

No amount of tarot cards, angel cards, or poker cards is going to do that. And remember, the angels aren't here to do that, either.

Yet people wander New Age stores looking for the next tool that will do the job, when in reality there's nothing that needs fixing. We're all children of God and all created perfectly in his image. You can't fix what isn't broken.

And no matter how often I say this, I still get calls and emails asking my opinion about one occult trapping or another. So, to continue with the list, let me briefly touch on the pendulum.

The last time I used a pendulum was when Archangel Gabriel first made contact with me. At the time, I was foolishly trying to connect with a spiritual mentor who had passed away months prior, but the pendulum didn't seem like it wanted to cooperate with my questioning that day. As I neared the end of a long yes/no session,

I heard a soft female voice calling my name. At first I thought it was my mentor, but I was quickly corrected.

"My name is Gabrielle." The voice seemed to flow all around me.

"Gabrielle who?" My brow arched as I looked about my empty bedroom. It was then that the archangel appeared to me and placed her hand upon mine, where the pendulum was swaying lazily.

"You don't need this. Put it away," she instructed, but my defenses went up immediately. I'd never seen this spirit before, and she was coming into my spiritual space uninvited.

"Who are you?" I asked again, ready for just about anything. I inched my hand toward a bag of sea salt, which is a great deterrent for unwanted spiritual energy.

"You know who I am, Chantel. And salt won't make me go away." She smiled knowingly.

I grumbled, "I only know of one Gabrielle and that's Archangel Gabriel. I thought he was a guy."

"Well, if you prefer that, I can make it so."

"Yeah, I prefer that." I looked her over with skeptical eyes.

The angel nodded politely and began to fade from my vision. "You don't need pendulums to connect with the realm of spirit, only your heart and pure intentions." I can't remember what I said in response to that, but I'm sure it was something smart-alecky.

Gabriel didn't return until later that night, and when he did, he wasn't wearing a soft, placating smile, but a stern glance that could rival an army general. (Lesson here: be careful what you ask for.) Our talk lasted a while, the main focus of it being my ability to connect with the angels—without the use of tools, of course. This was the conversation where he reminded me that JC had a job for me, the same job JC had proposed nearly a decade earlier. I wanted nothing to do with that job or with Gabriel, and had no qualms expressing this.

Needless to say, I lost that argument. But if I learned nothing else, I learned that we all have intuitive gifts, and such things as pendulums, crystal balls, scrying bowls, and tea leaves tend to get in the way, if not hamper our spiritual growth altogether.

After all, the power is in *you*, not the tools you're using.

Then there are the methods that offer theatrical results, but you might want to question whether they actually bring you closer to establishing a long-term relationship with the Divine. A connection may be established via these methods, but the chances of you connecting with an angel or ascended master are slim. Two methods that come instantly to mind are the planchette (the heart-shaped piece you use on a Ouija board) and table tipping.

I've had experience with both. And I have my reservations.

Now, some of you reading this are probably expecting me to say, "Stay away from Ouija boards! They only conjure up demons." That's not the case at all, actually. My reservation with the planchette, table tipping, and even pendulums, now that I've become a bit older and wiser, is that I believe they tend to attract energy that is more earthbound—in other words, the spirits of those who have yet to move on, for whatever reason, and are just looking for someone to talk to. That said, these spirits will say anything, and are either confused or in it for the thrill, much as you are. These spirits are looking for a bit of entertainment, which you provide with your squeals of excitement or screams of terror.

Could you contact Raphael through a pendulum? Probably. But why would you want to do that when he's willing to teach you how to connect with the angels without the use of such tools? After all, that pendulum's going to be pretty darn useless at thirty thousand feet if the plane's engines suddenly stall. I apologize for such a graphic and horrifying image, but the point is to drive home the importance of tapping into your own intuitive skills. Do that, and the only thing that can come between you and the comforting presence of your angels is *you*, something you have much more control over than, say, a planchette on a wobbling lap tray.

To sum it all up, these methods are fun and can be a great way to enjoy a night with the friends and family—heaven knows we need more togetherness in this age of computers, anonymity, and isolation. So don't be so quick to discard your tarot cards or I Ching set, as I think they provide great entertainment and even some cultural or historical insight into why people believe the way they do. But don't rely on these methods to fix your life or provide for you the wisdom you need to navigate your spiritual journey.

Get to know the angels for yourself and cut out these middleman methods. And yes, that even includes me—I won't take it personally. After all, I'm only here to show you how to connect with the angels. You're the one who has to engage them.

Frequently Asked Questions

The following FAQs may come up when you're experimenting with any methods of connecting with the angels, but they're particularly relevant when practicing clairaudience, clairsentience, claircognizance, and clairvoyance.

When I ask my angel a question, I don't receive a response.
The angels aren't ignoring you, so don't fret if on the first few tries you don't receive a message. Remember that these exercises are to help you discern which method you may be strongest in, and if after several attempts the angels still seem silent, experiment with the other methods until you get results.

Now, let's say you discover that you lean toward clairsentience. This doesn't mean that you should give up on clairaudience. Never hesitate to revisit a method or an exercise at a later date to see if the angels have opened up this channel to you. After all, they know best which methods you're most receptive to, and the order in which you should discover them.

What if my angel sounds (looks, feels) different than what is described in this book?
It's perfectly fine if Michael uses a gentle, poetic whisper instead of the boisterous contemporary colloquialisms I'm used to hearing from him. The angels will always present themselves in ways you are comfortable with. Furthermore, variations from what this book lists could also be attributed to your angel's way of introducing himself to you; when you feel more at ease talking to him, he may appear in a form that's closer to what's described in this book.

What if my validation sign doesn't manifest?
Because you may not always receive a validation in the next day or the next week, it's easy to become discouraged and believe that you were only having a conversation with yourself, not with the angels. Sometimes, signs of validation can take a

very long time to manifest, which is why I am so adamant about keeping these exercises playful and lighthearted.

Asking for validation, of course, is strictly about establishing contact with your angels, so don't be tempted to give up. Even if your sign doesn't appear, keep connecting with the angels. If the signs don't manifest after several attempts, explore other methods of connecting to see if another one will yield quicker results.

My validation sign appeared; what do I do now?

So, your sign manifested. You probably think you're ready to start barraging your angels with more hard-hitting questions, such as "So, just how much truth is there to *The Da Vinci Code*, anyhow?" Right? Well, not quite. You've still got a lot of training ahead of you.

Understand that the sign you receive not only validates the connection you had with your angels in that particular exercise, but indicates where your intuitive strengths lie. Continue practicing the exercises, seeking validation, and letting your angels guide you. Allow them to help you mature spiritually and prepare you for the moment when you're ready to discuss headier topics. Only your angels know when that moment will arrive, and when it does, they will most assuredly inform you.

Until then, don't hesitate to practice all the methods listed, to see if you can enhance your communication experience.

Helpful Hints for Using Clairvoyance and Dreams

The lists and discussions below address what you might "see" when interacting with an angel. Remember, of course, that all these symbols and icons are subjective. The Angel Code is the personal language you share with your angels; they will communicate with you in the ways that you best understand. And to better enhance your connection and receptivity, the angels may even guide you to make amendments to this section—so don't hesitate to make changes if something presented here doesn't feel right. Trust your intuition and make this book your own.

Angel Poses and Positions

The list below describes common poses that an angel may assume when connecting with you visually. As with humans, an angel's body language can speak volumes, enhancing the clarity of the message being conveyed.

YOUR ANGEL IS STANDING SHOULDER TO SHOULDER WITH YOU.

Your angel is reminding you that he's walking beside you. But this pose means even more than that, for if you are dealing with some sort of struggle at the time you connect with the angel, this stance is his way of saying he has faith in you as a reliable comrade on the battlefield. This is a time when you have to believe in yourself. Accept that you have the skills and strength to fight side-by-side with your angel—you're not some tiny, helpless human, but a very formidable contender against your adversaries. This position is a powerful one, because it's your angel's way of saying, "If this was a full-out war, I'd trust you to watch my back." Do not take this position lightly. The emphasis of this position is trust, in yourself as well as in your angel.

YOUR ANGEL IS WALKING AHEAD OF YOU.

This position indicates that your angel is guiding you to where you need to be. The road may prove arduous, but don't forget that your angel is leading you through obstacles—whatever obstacles you're supposed to face—for a reason. This journey is one of learning and self-discovery, so pay close attention to the details around you.

YOUR ANGEL IS STANDING BEFORE YOU, FACING YOU.

It's time to talk. Or, in a clairvoyant's world, it's time to play Pictionary. Your angel is asking for your attention at this point, and will start sending you visual messages soon. Grab your workbook and start writing down what you see, for later deciphering if needed. When the angel appears in this position, the images can range from the very specific to the very abstract. He could be holding his hands up, telling you to stop, or giving you two thumbs up in approval. He could also be handing you an item, or pointing to a blackboard upon which he might write or draw something.

Naturally, from a professional medium's perspective, this is the best position to see an angel in. It means that he's in a mood to chat; the more the angel conveys, the more information I can get for my client. On the other hand, it could also mean that the angel is about to pull down the infamous window shade. Archangel Raphael has appeared this way in plenty of consultations, then left me stammering because when he draws the window shade, it means he's not going to divulge a single thing.

There are many reasons why the angels won't answer specific questions, but one of the more common reasons is simply that the time isn't right for the question to be answered. Another common reason is that prior knowledge of a situation could lead to more headache and heartache. For example, if one of my clients knew ahead of time that her spouse was going to serve her with divorce papers, she'd be doing everything within her power to launch a preemptive strike. Well, in her case, doing so would prove even more disastrous than remaining reactionary, because no matter what she did, the outcome is set in stone. Trying to intercept or divert God's will only leaves us weary and winded.

The client might have an inkling of a possible divorce, but the angels are mum on the subject, focusing instead on her health. They encourage her to get ample rest and make sure that her house is in order. Needless to say, when she can't get an answer to her main question, she's probably none too happy with me or the angels.

It's not easy for me as a medium in this respect, since I have a deep and genuine interest in helping my clients navigate life with the help of the angels. And while I fully understand that sometimes no answer *is* the answer, trying to get someone who may not be as angel-savvy to understand this can be daunting, to say the least. After all, the angels will only tell us what we need to know, not what we want to know.

YOUR ANGEL IS WALKING BEHIND YOU.

Right now, your angel is taking a passive role and allowing you to go about your journey without any input from him. I've seen this position many times, and nothing seems to be more frustrating than wanting an angel's guidance only to find him hanging back as you bumble and trip your way along. The angel isn't doing this to be cruel, though—he's allowing you a moment of self-discovery.

Believe it or not, the answers we often seek from our angels are already contained within us. The angels, in their vast wisdom, know whether speaking or silence will be the best teaching tool, so don't beleaguer them with demands. If they're not conveying anything, just go about business as usual. Eventually, when the time is right, they'll send some visual communication your way.

YOUR ANGEL IS STANDING BEHIND YOU.

This is a position of support and comfort. Whenever I see an angel standing in this position with a client, I know that the client is in a time of mourning or going through a serious crisis, one that usually involves a loss of some sort. If there is distance between my client and her angel, however, it immediately tells me that she's not willing to listen to what the angel has to say and will only be receptive to what she wants to hear. This goes back to the issue of surrender and detaching oneself from desired results. Don't allow your desire to have things be a certain way build a wall between you and your angels and guides. As the mothers of the church I once attended used to say, "Let go and let God."

Your angel may wrap his arms around you to comfort you. He may even wrap his wings around you. Either way, let yourself melt into the moment and feel the closeness—this is your angel's way of letting you know that he understands what you're going through, and that he's there to offer a shoulder to cry on. His wings will protect you from all the fears that may be roiling through you at the moment. This is an intensely warm, loving, and sheltering position, one to be welcomed when you find yourself in that darkest hour.

YOUR ANGEL IS CRADLING OR CARRYING YOU.

This is another position of comfort and protection, but it also represents healing and transition. Allowing yourself to be carried by someone is a gesture of trust; when you see yourself in the arms of your angel, know that healing is on the way. Just as importantly, this position can portend a significant life shift—be prepared, for the life you once knew may be ending. Yet fear not, for a new beginning is upon you. This whole notion may seem frightening, but remember that your angel is literally carrying you through this. Trust in him and in your Creator, and know that everything that happens is a part of God's Great Equation. If you couldn't handle it, you wouldn't be going through it to begin with.

Visual Cues

If you work with your angels on a regular basis, you'll get to know them so well that you'll recognize them no matter what form they take. And to help you better understand the messages they're conveying when they visually appear, I've drawn up a list of common images that the angels have used during my consultations. Keep in mind, this list is short and general for a reason—as you work with the angels, you're going to eventually create a visual database that is uniquely your own. So, as the angels present new images, don't overanalyze; just follow your first thought. (In chapter 3, each angel's entry includes space for you to add your own visual cues. But until you build your personal database, here are some images to get you started.)

ARENA

EMPTY: It's just you and your angel in the arena, and it's training season. Expect internal changes (shifts in how you view yourself, your friends, the world, etc.).

FULL: You've got spectators and the game is on. Go forth and give it the old college try. The angels are rooting for you!

BEACH

This is Michael's way of saying that it's time to rest and have a little fun. Take a vacation and leave your work at work.

CAVE

I often call this the "healing cave." This is where Raphael—and most likely two Native American or Aboriginal spirit guides—will meet with you to perform a healing and/or purification ceremony. In the ceiling of this cave is a skylight, through which God's holy light beams down. You may be asked to sit or lie within this beam of light while Raphael and his helpers perform their tasks.

Seeing the image of a cave indicates that now, more than ever, is a time for you to seek rest and meditation to help your mind and body heal. Many clients who have received this cue have said to me, "Wow, but I feel fine," only to wind up flat on their back days later. So don't take this cue with a grain of salt. Work with your doctor to keep yourself in tip-top shape, and make sure that stress is kept at a minimum.

CHILDREN'S GAMES

Sandalphon is in the foreground, urging you to tap into your inner child and allow yourself time for play and laughter. Have a fun pillow fight, go to a baseball game, visit a carnival, or draw on your sidewalk with chalk—whatever it takes. The point is that you're in need of healing, and laughter is the medicine this angel is prescribing.

DOLPHIN

This is one of Raphael's many signs that indicate spiritual healing is underway.

DOVE

Raphael usually gives this visual to ask you to seek a peaceful and calm approach to your situation. This also indicates that he is bringing his own soothing presence into your life, and that this is a time for quiet reflection.

LION

This is Michael's symbol, indicating that he is present and protecting you. There is nothing to fear.

LOTUS

This is a time for meditation and self-discovery.

MOON

FULL: This is a time of magic and discovery. New knowledge is approaching.

NEW: This is a time for stillness and reflection.

RED: Beware the ego that often comes with newfound spiritual growth. Just because you're enlightened doesn't mean you can look down upon those who haven't quite gotten to where you are just yet.

OCEAN (BODIES OF WATER)

ROCKY: Turbulent emotions are only going to worsen matters.

CALM: This is a time to relax and reflect on your current situation.

RAINBOW

This is a time of happiness. Allow your inner child to come out and play for a while!

ROSE

PINK: Mother's love; divine love.

RED: Romantic love.

YELLOW: Happiness; friendship; apology.

BLACK (WITHERED): Significant transition.

WHITE: Surrender; pure intentions.

SCROLL

Gabriel often uses this visual to indicate he's coming into someone's life as a mentoring angel, to take them to their next spiritual level in this lifetime.

SNOW GLOBE (SHAKEN)

Michael usually uses this visual to warn you that the environment you live in is about to undergo significant change (change in employment, housing, family/friend dynamics, etc.).

VOLCANO

It's time to take a warrior's stance and stand up for what you believe in.

A Note on Angel Icons and Physical Appearance

If you look at angels in art—from Michelangelo to that pretty angel card deck you might have sitting on your bookshelf—you'll notice that the accepted Western image of angels really hasn't changed much over time. Angels are usually portrayed as human figures dressed in white robes or medieval battle armor, with feathered wings, halos, swords, trumpets, or even harps. These symbols and their connotations are rooted in the ancient cultures of Babylon and Egypt, long before Judaism, Christianity, and Islam came onto the scene. The white robes symbolize light, holiness, and purity; the wings and halos, which were common among the ancient Egyptian gods, are symbols of divinity. Musical instruments have been considered symbols of the angels' unyielding praise of God, while swords, and later, battle armor, represent cosmic and spiritual warfare, as well as God's wrath manifest.

As I worked more and more with the archangels, however, I came to realize that not all of them subscribe to traditional Western iconography. Not all of the archangels flash big billowy wings. Not all of the angels wear white. And not all of them wear robes and sandals. Rather, each angel has his own set of icons.

You'll notice that in the Angelic Associations entries in chapter 3, while I describe what the angels wear, I don't prescribe what they physically look like. I don't list hair color or eye color or even skin color, because the angels will appear to each of us differently. They'll incarnate in ways we're comfortable with. As an angel medium, I've been able to see the angels in different manifestations. Since they don't often change appearance when visiting me *for* me, whenever they do appear with a new look, I consider it a sign that at some point in a consultation, my client is going to ask, "So, what does my angel look like, anyway?"

One time, for example, Michael threw me completely off balance in the middle of a consultation. To me, this general of the angelic armies appears as a tall, buff, tan blond with vibrant green eyes. When I tell people this, I've gotten all sorts of responses ranging from "Wow, really? That's nothing like what I envision" to "That's exactly how I see him." But during this very memorable consultation, Michael strutted into the room in a form that made me look twice. If it weren't for his energy signature, I might not have recognized him. His tunic was ripped away, and he was wearing only his white skirting. Gone was his sword, as well as his blond hair. And his tan had deepened—by about five shades. Before me was a Michael with skin the color of deep, rich chocolate. His head was bare and he toted a javelin that made him look every bit the ancient African warrior. To say the least, he was as beautiful in this form as in the other form I was used to seeing, but unfortunately, it caused a huge dilemma for me.

My client was Caucasian.

And this is where our human "junk" can get in the way of our spiritual growth. I was sweating bullets the entire consultation, praying she wouldn't ask me what Michael looked like. I simply didn't know how she would feel about having an ebony archangel by her side. Well, the inevitable happened—she finally asked. I took a deep breath, gritted my teeth, and glared at Michael, who merely grinned back at me.

"Well," I said, wincing, "you know that angels often take on forms we're comfortable with, so he can be whatever you want him to be." I was doing my best to hedge, but my starry-eyed client was insistent. Admittedly, the consultation had gone well up to that point, as she had validated much of what the angels were saying. Needless to say, because of this she was eager to finally meet them for herself.

My eyes darted back up to Michael, who was standing behind her looking like an African Mr. Clean, and I just wanted to punch him for putting me in such an uncomfortable position. But I knew better than to filter or censor anything that was coming across the spiritual channels, and with the way my client was pressing to know what her warrior angel looked like, I had no choice but to tell her the truth.

I was not at all prepared for her reaction. I was ready for her to scoff and accuse me of projecting my own perceptions into her reading, but that wasn't the case. Never in all the years I've given consultations have I seen anyone smile as wide as this woman did that day. Her cheeks flushed, her eyes twinkled, and she glanced over her shoulder a moment before returning her gaze to me.

"Really? Are you serious?" she said. I couldn't chisel that grin off her face.

But I still felt tense and tried to downplay it. "Well, as I said, he can take any form you find appealing…"

Her hands sprung up, interrupting my nervous back-pedalling, and then she leaned into the table to whisper to me, "Trust me, Chantel, you just made my day."

My jaw nearly hit the table. I sat back with a sigh of relief and chuckled dryly, first at her reaction and then at my own fear that she'd find the information offensive.

Naturally, this says more about me than anything else, and from that day on, I stopped questioning the angels and second-guessing myself in a consultation. Whatever they channel, that's what I report, whether it makes me feel uncomfortable or not. After all, it's not about me, it's about my client.

Beyond the superficial things such as skin color and physical appearance, the angels can also switch gender. As I've mentioned, when Gabriel first came to me, he was in his female form, but my life circumstances at the time just wouldn't allow me to listen to a female authority figure. So he shifted to his male form.

I've also seen Michael in his female form—she reminds me of a red-headed Xena who could singlehandedly put a hurting on Sparta, Persia, and all the warriors in between. Pair her up with another hot-tempered warrior angel, like Uriel, and we could very well have an apocalypse on our hands. Where Michael's male form is sunny, bright, and jovial, his female side is fierce and deadly. Frankly, she makes me shudder just thinking about her, but some of my clients have her as a mentoring angel, and rightfully so. One memorable client who has her is an activist for women's rights. Another is a female police officer from New York City.

But I'll pass on Xena and keep the sun-kissed model of male physical perfection, thank you. That's what I'm comfortable with, and I'm sticking to it.

Because the angels can change their appearance at the drop of a hat, then, it's good for those who rely on clairvoyance or dreams to take note of their angels' icons, visual cues, and body language. Even though I drew on clairsentience to learn that the ebony angel in the consultation was Michael, there were also visual clues that I could have used had my empathetic skills been lacking that day. For example, the polearm that Michael carried was a dead giveaway. While this is not one of his usual icons today, we have to remember that Michael, above all things, is a warrior angel—this is how he carried himself when he entered the room. Another clue to his identity was the signature ripped tunic. You can count on Michael to show just how able he is to lead the angelic armies into battle. And a last clue, which couldn't be mistaken, was his sunny smile.

It helps to document the icons you come across when visually connecting with your angels, so that you'll be able to recognize that angel's presence no matter what form it takes. After all, an altered appearance or form can provide further clues to the message the angel is trying to convey.

3

ANGELIC ASSOCIATIONS

IN THIS CHAPTER, YOU'LL MEET sixteen archangels. The entries that follow are based on my experiences with these particular angels (along with research and the experiences of my clients and students), and contain factoids ranging from historical descriptions to more modern insights (an angel's scent type, for example). For those of you who have read *Azrael Loves Chocolate*, the format of these entries may seem a bit familiar; I've repeated it here in order to expand upon the information presented in my first book.

As you get to know these benevolent beings of light, of course, you'll develop your own language for speaking with them. You'll discover the signs and symbols that constitute your unique Angel Code. Therefore, I've included blank spaces at the end of each angel's entry where you can add your own associations. You can also work with the information already in the entries, circling or striking out items that resonate or don't resonate with you. My goal, in presenting these entries, is to help you decipher your angels' messages while you are first learning how to communicate with them.

At the end of each angel's section is a brief discussion of what you might encounter when dealing with that particular angel through clairaudience, clairsentience, clairvoyance, and dreams.

But not claircognizance, you'll note.

The reason why I don't include claircognizants in each discussion is that those of you who connect with the angels through claircognizance do so by tapping directly into the akashic records. While people who draw on the other methods of connection will have varying types of experiences and successes connecting with each angel, the only difference claircognizants will experience, when working with one angel or another, is that they will *channel* the information differently. That is to say, you'll glean the exact same information from Heaven's database each time, but the angel you're talking to may filter the knowledge in different ways. You will thus find yourself closely reflecting the angel's demeanor (as you perceive it).

For example, if you connect with Cassiel, you will probably feel emboldened and use the information you receive to vie for the underdog and fight for those who are helpless. The same information, channeled through Azrael, may cause you to approach the situation with quiet poise and grace. Information channeled through Gabriel may move you to utilize diplomacy and engage others through the art of speaking and writing.

Your connection to the akashic records, through the personality of your angel, will not only provide you with abundant insight, but also with the wisdom of how best to apply it.

Archangel Ariel

MEANING OF NAME: *Lion of God.*

PATRON ANGEL OF: Activism, adventurers, animals and pets, campers, ecology, healers, meteorology, park rangers, veterinarians, zoology.

ADDITIONAL NAMES/AVATARS: Arael, Ariael.

HEAVENLY ASSIGNMENT: The ever sassy and quick-witted Ariel watches over the balance and health of nature along with Archangel Chamuel. She helps us to connect and harmonize with all of Creation while at the same time serving as a muse who opens our eyes to the breathtaking beauty and fierceness of nature.

USUALLY ARRIVES IN YOUR LIFE: When you feel you've few tools to work through your life circumstances, Ariel appears to inspire innovation and invention through necessity. She teaches us to use (and reuse) what we already have at our disposal without having to seek out additional resources.

PROMOTES/EVOKES: Ambition, compassion, conservation, determination, fairness, honesty, innovation, integrity, motivation, trust, vivaciousness.

DIFFUSES: Deception, greed, hopelessness, hoarding, subterfuge, feelings of inadequacy and lack.

ENERGY SIGNATURE (TEMPERATURE/SPEED/ELEMENT): Cool/Varies/Water.

ASCENDED MASTERS WITH SIMILAR ENERGY SIGNATURES: Coventina, Dana, Glooscap, Maahes, Maeve, Sedna.

WINGS: White/light gray.

USUAL ATTIRE: While Ariel's demeanor is quite lively, like Iophiel's, this archangel passed up brightly colored attire to match her brother Cassiel. While she's not one to dress in a leather biker jacket, she's partial to street clothing that expresses her larger-than-life 'tude. When she first appeared to me, she was dressed in layers of black and gray, with all kinds of jingly things attached to a jacket worn over a hoodie. And as one of the most petite angels I've ever met, she also looks quite young—in her late teens at best. With big bright eyes, a beautiful smile, and a tongue sharper than Michael's, she can hold her own around the big boys.

ICONS: Javelin, jewels, lion's head, sword and shield, wind.

ANIMALS: All, but especially bear, cheetah, hawk, horse, lion, raven, zebra.

VEGETATION: Apple, carrot, garlic, grass, pepper plant, pine nut.

OBJECTS: Conservation areas, forests, lakes, open fields, valleys, the weather.

PLANET: Uranus.

DAY: Tuesday.

SEASONS: Summer/fall.

BASIC ELEMENT: Water.

METALS: Pewter, silver.

CRYSTALS & GEMSTONES: Aventurine, crystal quartz, emerald.

SHAPES: Steep waves.

CHAKRAS: Root, heart.

MUSICAL NOTE: E.

MUSICAL INSTRUMENTS: Bagpipes, banjo, flute, guitar.

COLORS: Jewel tones.

NUMERICAL VIBRATION: 3.

SCENTS: Apple, musk, pine.

SCENT TYPE: Earthy.

CLOTHING (TEXTILE): Denim and cotton.

YOUR PERSONAL ASSOCIATIONS, VISUAL CUES, AND NOTES:

_____

_____

_____

_____

_____

_____

Connecting with Ariel

Archangel Ariel is always up for good conversation. She's quite savvy about current events and pop culture, so **clairaudients** should have no difficulty finding something casual to chat about. She is always happy to share her insights, with a wit and humor that will surely keep you giggling the rest of the day. If you ever need a pep talk or someone to bring a little sunlight into an otherwise overcast day, Ariel's your angel.

Clairsentients will find Ariel's presence to be cool and calming, and one of the best places to connect with her is out in nature. She loves nature trails, hiking, and camping.

Clairvoyants and **dreamers** may be a bit surprised when they see Ariel. According to many historical texts, Ariel is male, but that's not the way she appeared to me. And from what I can sense, she's not changing that any time soon.

Ariel may seem petite, but she can tangle with the best of opponents. "I'm wiry," she grinned at me, from beneath a wild mane of hair.

Though I've yet to see Ariel assume animal form, she informed me that she does it quite often and will appear to many as an animal guide. So don't be so quick to discount the horse that appears in your visions. It could be Archangel Ariel.

However she appears to you, you can always expect Ariel's demeanor to be playful and uplifting.

Archangel Azrael

MEANING OF NAME: *God Helps*.

PATRON ANGEL OF: Death, the dying and the dead, caretakers, morticians, grief counselors, funeral home directors; also watches over pallbearers to secure their steps in a procession.

ADDITIONAL NAMES/AVATARS: Ashriel, Azaril, Azrail, Azriel, the Angel of Death.

HEAVENLY ASSIGNMENT: Any angel or group of angels may arrive to assist us with the transition from this world to the next, but it is Azrael who is assigned the task of retrieving those of us who struggle and try to cling to life when our time here on the Earthly plane has expired. Azrael is known, and rightly so, as the Angel of

Death, and the gruesome stigma that follows him is only because he is the one who has to carry souls off kicking and screaming. Still, he does so with compassion and love and the desire to help souls transition into their new existence. Some of us will accept death willingly when it comes. Some of us may fear it, yet surrender quietly just the same. In that case, we can expect to see our angels and guides, as well as our loved ones who have passed on before us. For the rest of us, clawing at the bedpost and digging our heels into the ground, there's the tall and dark Azrael. (He's not as scary as he sounds; after all, he likes chocolate and classic black and white movies!)

USUALLY ARRIVES IN YOUR LIFE: Azrael doesn't show up only when death is near, so don't flip out on him when he appears. This archangel helps us when we're struggling with our fears of death and the unknown. He will come to comfort those who simply aren't sure what's awaiting them on the other side, as well as to give you glimpses into existence in the realm of spirit. Azrael is not an angel to be feared, but embraced as a gentle and loving guide who wishes that everyone would welcome him with open arms. After all, he's the one accompanying us on the last leg home when we're too weary or afraid to make it on our own.

PROMOTES/EVOKES: Feelings of companionship, peace, security.

DIFFUSES: Desperation, grief, guilt, hopelessness, loneliness, regret, unworthiness, woe.

ENERGY SIGNATURE (TEMPERATURE/SPEED/ELEMENT): Cool/Varies/Aether.

ASCENDED MASTERS WITH SIMILAR ENERGY SIGNATURES: Charon, Enma, Kali, Yama.

WINGS: Black mottled with dove gray.

USUAL ATTIRE: Black billowing robes of satin; white robes of linen.*

ICONS: Raven, scythe, skull/skeleton.

ANIMALS: Bat, beetle, crow, dragon, moth and butterfly, raven, vulture.

---

* Note: Azrael's attire and icons are not omens of death, but merely indications of Azrael's presence, which helps us to deal with our fears of death. These are also symbols of significant life transitions.

VEGETATION: Cypress, hemlock (poison), lily, yew (poison).

OBJECTS: Cemetery, death shroud, flocks of singing/squawking birds, grave, scythe, skull/skeleton.

PLANETS: Saturn, Pluto.

DAY: Saturday.

SEASONS: Fall, winter.

BASIC ELEMENT: Aether.

METALS: Cinnabar (poison), lead (poison), mercury (poison).

CRYSTALS & GEMSTONES: Black tourmaline.

SHAPES: Smooth waves.

CHAKRA: Crown.

MUSICAL NOTE: F.

MUSICAL INSTRUMENTS: Cello, harpsichord.

COLORS: Black, gray, silver, white.

NUMERICAL VIBRATION: 0.

SCENT: Lily.

SCENT TYPE: Heavy floral.

CLOTHING (TEXTILE): Satin.

YOUR PERSONAL ASSOCIATIONS, VISUAL CUES, AND NOTES:

_____

_____

_____

_____

Connecting with Azrael

Azrael brings with him an immense sense of peace and comfort when he visits. For the **clairaudient**, his voice is deep and soulful; it flows like rhythmic poetry that lures you in. It's soft, almost breathy on the ears.

To the **clairsentient**, Azrael's presence is cool—a breath of fresh air accented by the scent of flowers and rain.

To the **clairvoyant**, Azrael may seem intimidating with his billowing black robes and a scythe, but he'll know whether or not you can handle these images. If you're among the faint of heart, he may appear instead as soft, rolling storm clouds, or he may send his black mare, Duchess, to prance about playfully until you feel at ease with his presence.

Dreams of death do not necessarily portend death, but indicate significant transitions in life. So, if you have a nightmare about someone dying—or even your own death—call on Azrael for comfort and insight as to what the dream could mean for you.

Archangel Cassiel

MEANING OF NAME: *Speed of God.*

PATRON ANGEL OF: The downtrodden, the enslaved, the impoverished, the oppressed, the unjustly persecuted, orphaned children.

ADDITIONAL NAMES/AVATARS: Casiel, Casziel, Kafziel.

HEAVENLY ASSIGNMENT: Known as the Angel of Tears, Cassiel offers his quiet presence to those in need of comfort during their most sorrowful moments.

USUALLY ARRIVES IN YOUR LIFE: When you are at your darkest hour, feeling abandoned by all that you held dear. When your heart is heaviest and overflowing with tears, Cassiel appears to help shoulder the burden of your woes and keep at bay feelings of hopelessness.

PROMOTES/EVOKES: Activism, courage, faith, fortitude, restraint, tranquility, uniqueness.

DIFFUSES: Angst, defeat, desolation, disgust, isolation, guilt, loathing, rage, regret, solitude, sorrow.

ENERGY SIGNATURE (TEMPERATURE/SPEED/ELEMENT): Cool/Rapid/Water.

ASCENDED MASTERS WITH SIMILAR ENERGY SIGNATURES: Osiris. For the most part, Cassiel accompanies all of Heaven's manifestations to lend a helping hand anywhere and everywhere he can.

WINGS: Dark gray to blue-black.

USUAL ATTIRE: Prefers street clothing. Black denim jeans, combat or biker boots, muscle shirt, and leather biker jacket or leather trench. His formal attire is usually a burgundy tunic, leather breeches, and a navy or gray cloak.

ICONS: Dragon, full moon, raven, sword.

ANIMALS: Crow, dragon, koi, raven, snow leopard, snowy owl, sparrow, spider, vulture.

VEGETATION: Beet, belladonna (poison), garlic, henbane (poison), holly, nightshade family (poison), patchouli, pumpkin, snapdragon, straw, turnip.

OBJECTS: Anime, cemeteries, cityscapes, crypts, dreamscape, mausoleums, moon and moonlight, nighttime, old church buildings, rain, swords (especially a nihontō).

PLANET: Saturn.

DAY: Saturday.

SEASONS: Fall, winter.

BASIC ELEMENT: Water.

METAL: Lead (poison).

CRYSTALS & GEMSTONES: Agate, crystal quartz, hematite, jasper, kunzite, pyrite.

SHAPES: Sharp spiky formations, yin-yang.

CHAKRAS: Root, throat.

MUSICAL NOTE: A.

MUSICAL INSTRUMENTS: Bass guitar; synthesizer (anything digitized, computerized, etc.).

COLORS: Black.

NUMERICAL VIBRATION: 0.

SCENT: Patchouli.

SCENT TYPES: Leather, musk.

CLOTHING (TEXTILE): Leather, wool.

YOUR PERSONAL ASSOCIATIONS, VISUAL CUES, AND NOTES:

_____

_____

_____

_____

_____

_____

Connecting with Cassiel

Dreamscape is Cassiel's preferred mode of communication, and when it comes to making his presence known, he leaves little to guesswork. Those connecting with this beautiful, mysterious angel will find themselves dreaming of him frequently. You may dream of seeing him standing on a busy city street at night, or in a crowd, or even as your own reflection in a mirror. Regardless of where you see him in your dreams, he will often appear against the backdrop of nighttime, one of his primary elements and a time when many of us feel the most vulnerable.

Cassiel is known for having a striking appearance, and many of my clients who have encountered him initially thought they were dreaming of ghosts, vampires, or werewolves, yet no one reported feeling threatened by these images. This is Cassiel's *modus operandi*—to use his appearance as a way of letting us know that exteriors mean little in the grander scheme of things. What matters most is what dwells inside us all.

Beneath the strange guises, Cassiel is a beautiful, vibrant angel of God who shares the burdens of all our sorrows. To the **clairaudient**, he may not have much to say until you've established a rapport through your dreams. He speaks very softly, and you can expect him to use modern colloquialisms or even street slang on occasion.

For the **clairsentient**, Cassiel feels like a chilly October night while sitting by a bonfire. His presence is comforting, but there are intermittent moments of cold, brisk air that invigorates more than chills.

I urge the **clairvoyant** to be as open-minded as possible, for Cassiel looks nothing like the angel archetypes many of us are used to seeing in books and angel art. I know I've said that the angels will appear in ways that are comfortable for us, but Cassiel is the very rare exception. His purpose may be to shoulder the woes of the world, but he is also a teacher of tolerance and acceptance. As a result, he won't trade in his black attire to please anyone. He's a rebel, too, if you hadn't noticed, and he's here to help all of us look past the surface and into the soul.

Archangel Chamuel

MEANING OF NAME: *He Who Sees [Seeks] God.*

PATRON ANGEL OF: Chefs and cooks, emergency aid workers, environmentalists, farmers, fitness trainers, forest rangers, gardeners, horticulturists, hunters (non-recreational) and gatherers, naturalists, outdoor survivalists, philanthropists, protectors and preservationists of nature, warriors.

ADDITIONAL NAMES/AVATARS: Kamuel, Simiel.

HEAVENLY ASSIGNMENT: Chamuel is a mild-mannered angel who oversees the balance and order of Nature. He is also instrumental in helping humankind to understand its connection with the planet Earth.

USUALLY ARRIVES IN YOUR LIFE: When you are facing challenges of staying true to yourself and your cause.

PROMOTES/EVOKES: Balance, clarity, compassion, empathy, harmony, serenity, tolerance.

DIFFUSES: Anxiety, apathy, hysteria, imbalance, panic.

ENERGY SIGNATURE (TEMPERATURE/SPEED/ELEMENT): Warm/Even/Earth.

ASCENDED MASTERS WITH SIMILAR ENERGY SIGNATURES: Abundantia, Áine, Artemis, Babaji, Butterfly Maiden, Diana, Gaia, Green Man, Kokopelli, Pan, St. Francis, Taras (Green and White), Vila.

WINGS: Brown wings of an eagle.

USUAL ATTIRE: Usually wears a cloak of dark brown or hunter green. May take on the form of the Green Man, a Buddhist monk, a shaman, a Native American warrior, or an Aboriginal elder.

ICONS: Bamboo staff, lotus flower, stag.

ANIMALS: All living creatures, but especially the goat, preying mantis, stag.

VEGETATION: Bamboo, bodhi, coconut, corn, cucumber, ginger, henna, ivy, jasmine, lilac, lotus, maple, oak, orchid, pea, peony, pine, pumpkin, rice, sweetgrass, tea, tobacco, witch hazel.

OBJECTS: Earth, foliage, forests, trees, mountains, nature retreats, thunderstorms, tribal art.

PLANETS: Jupiter, Neptune.

DAY: Thursday.

SEASON: Spring.

BASIC ELEMENT: Earth.

METALS: Pewter, tin.

CRYSTALS & GEMSTONES: Agate, amber, crystal quartz, peridot.

SHAPES: Egg shapes, ovals, yin-yang.

CHAKRA: Heart.

MUSICAL NOTE: E.

MUSICAL INSTRUMENT: Tribal drums.

COLORS: Earth tones.

NUMERICAL VIBRATION: 3.

SCENTS: Coconut, cucumber, ginger, jasmine, lilac, lotus, maple, peony, pine, sweet-grass, Nag Champa, ylang-ylang.

SCENT TYPES: Exotic, woodsy.

CLOTHING (TEXTILE): Wool.

YOUR PERSONAL ASSOCIATIONS, VISUAL CUES, AND NOTES:

_____

_____

_____

_____

_____

_____

Connecting with Chamuel

Those who practice yoga or meditation on a regular basis will find connecting with Chamuel to be relatively easy. No matter where your intuitive strengths lie, Chamuel connects best with those who can quiet the mind and practice the art of stillness.

The **clairvoyant** and **dreamer** will usually find Chamuel meditating in his garden, while the **clairsentient** will feel a sense of tranquility and otherworldliness (dare I say, even a feeling akin to an out-of-body experience).

The **clairaudient** will quickly discover that Chamuel usually answers a question with a question, if not a metaphor, parable, or even a riddle or two. Deep thinkers will enjoy long conversations with Chamuel, for he is an angel who is focused on human growth, discovery, and enlightenment.

Archangel Gabriel

MEANING OF NAME: *God Is My Strength.*

PATRON ANGEL OF: Actors, bloggers, computer (gadget) geeks, entrepreneurs, journalists, life coaches, motivational speakers, orators, philosophers, physicists, poets, sacred geometry, theologians, writers.

ADDITIONAL NAMES/AVATARS: Jibril (Islamic), the Man in Linen.

HEAVENLY ASSIGNMENT: Gabriel is the mediator between human beings and God. He is the chief of all messengers.

USUALLY ARRIVES IN YOUR LIFE: When you begin to question your place in God's Great Equation and want to take a conscious role in fulfilling your life's purpose.

PROMOTES/EVOKES: Discovery, duty, elation, inspiration, joy, motivation, patience, propriety, restraint.

DIFFUSES: Feelings of annoyance, boredom, complacency, frustration, inadequacy, unworthiness.

ENERGY SIGNATURE (TEMPERATURE/SPEED/ELEMENT): Hot/Rapid/Air.

ASCENDED MASTERS WITH SIMILAR ENERGY SIGNATURES: Confucius, Jesus, Mother Mary Queen of Angels, St. Germain, Siddhartha Gautama Buddha.

WINGS: Off-white/beige with threads of gold.

USUAL ATTIRE: Draping white linen robes and gold sandals. (Rumor has it that he has wings on his sandals—like the Greek god Mercury—but I've yet to see them. I think Michael's just joking on that one.)

ICONS: Banner, scroll, sword, trumpet.

ANIMALS: Chameleon, giraffe, grasshopper, gull, horse, rhinoceros, robin, sparrow, starling.

VEGETATION: Almond, anise, bergamot (orange), bleeding heart, bodhi, cedar, cinquefoil, dandelion, eyebright, fern, grain, holly, hops, ivy, mint, olive, papyrus, pistachio, rose, sage, slippery elm.

OBJECTS: Angel art, communications (radio waves, fiber optics, etc.), images of angel choirs, mountains, paper scrolls (declarations/decrees), swords, theater (stage), wind.

PLANETS: Moon, Uranus.

DAY: Monday.

SEASON: Summer.

BASIC ELEMENT: Air.

METALS: Copper, gold, lead, silver.

CRYSTALS & GEMSTONES: Agate, azurite, citrine, crystal quartz, rutilated quartz, sapphire.

SHAPES: Lune, straight lines.

CHAKRAS: Solar plexus, throat, third eye.

MUSICAL NOTE: D.

MUSICAL INSTRUMENTS: Brass instruments (especially the trumpet).

COLORS: Cream, gold, white, yellow.

NUMERICAL VIBRATION: 3.

SCENTS: Almond, anise, bergamot (orange), cedar, mint, rose, sage.

SCENT TYPES: Cool, airy, clean.

CLOTHING (TEXTILE): Linen.

YOUR PERSONAL ASSOCIATIONS, VISUAL CUES, AND NOTES:

_____

_____

_____

_____

_____

_____

Connecting with Gabriel

As I've said many times before, Gabriel is quite stringent. As messenger of messengers, he will make sure that **clairaudients** understand everything he has to say. Firm, direct, and succinct, Gabriel can make those he connects with feel like they're in boot camp. He doesn't mince words, and will often reinforce his instructions by sending signs on a regular basis.

To the **clairsentient**, Gabriel's presence may feel a bit overwhelming at first because he has a larger-than-life aura that precedes him. I sometimes liken him to a shrewd and demanding scholar … from the Renaissance period.

Gabriel's form may make the **clairvoyant** and **dreamer** sit up and take notice. With his straight back and purposeful strides, it's hard to mistake the Man in Linen for anything less than commanding. Upon first meeting the angel, you may have difficulty gazing directly at him, for his eyes seem to pierce the soul and observe what lies at the core of your being. His very presence alone will make you think, "Am I being honest with myself?"

Archangel Haniel

MEANING OF NAME: *Grace of God.*

PATRON ANGEL OF: Astrology, astronomy, charity workers, clergy, diplomats, healers, intuitives, light workers, relief workers.

ADDITIONAL NAMES/AVATARS: Aniel, Hamiel, Hanael, Onoel.

HEAVENLY ASSIGNMENT: Haniel is a ministering angel who carries within him the love and grace of God, and brings healing and succor to those with a troubled spirit.

USUALLY ARRIVES IN YOUR LIFE: When you find yourself feeling unworthy of God's benevolence and are mired in destructive emotions, Haniel steps in to help soothe the soul, ease the mind, and bring messages of blessings and forgiveness.

PROMOTES/EVOKES: Compassion, composure, consideration, discretion, gentleness, inclusion, love, self-respect.

DIFFUSES: Depression, despair, doubt, guilt, self-sabotage/destruction, uselessness, worthlessness.

ENERGY SIGNATURE (TEMPERATURE/SPEED/ELEMENT): Warm/Slow/Air.

ASCENDED MASTERS WITH SIMILAR ENERGY SIGNATURES: St. John of God, Spider Grandmother, Yarkhibol.

WINGS: White.

USUAL ATTIRE: Haniel's not picky about attire. I've seen him don white robes like his brother Gabriel, but I've also seen him don a brown leather and suede getup that made him look like he was pulled straight off the North American Plains during the 1800s. And yes, he was wearing a cowboy hat. (I've no idea why—when he appears to me, he has the most beautiful head of long, chestnut hair I've ever seen on a male.)

ICONS: Angel wings, heart of compassion, rainbow, sunbeams, white dove.

ANIMALS: Deer, dove, sparrow.

VEGETATION: Bleeding heart, cinquefoil, cotton, holly, olive, peace lily, palm, rose, sage.

OBJECTS: Astral bodies, lantern, symbols of peace, wreath.

PLANETS: Moon, Venus.

DAY: Monday, Friday.

SEASON: Fall.

BASIC ELEMENT: Air.

METALS: Gold, platinum.

CRYSTALS & GEMSTONES: Crystal quartz, jade, rose quartz, sodalite.

SHAPES: Lune, pentacle.

CHAKRA: Heart.

MUSICAL NOTE: G.

MUSICAL INSTRUMENTS: Tapping toes and clapping hands.

COLORS: Muted earth tones.

NUMERICAL VIBRATION: 5.

SCENTS: Rose, sage.

SCENT TYPES: Subtle, clean, airy.

CLOTHING (TEXTILE): Linen.

YOUR PERSONAL ASSOCIATIONS, VISUAL CUES, AND NOTES:

_____

_____

_____

_____

Connecting with Haniel

I've found Archangel Haniel to be just as capable at quick comebacks and witty remarks as his brother Michael. When I saw the two together one evening, they were like old friends who enjoy bantering back and forth in a battle of comical cleverness.

Clairaudients connecting with Haniel will find him to be easygoing, laid-back, and willing to discuss just about anything. Nothing seems to faze this angel—not even Michael. His presence is all about peace, calmness, and divine love, so allow yourself to bask in his warmth and listen to his words of encouragement as he channels them straight from the Throne, straight from the heart of God.

Clairsentients will simply feel aglow in the presence of this graceful angel. Haniel offers strength to the weak, hope to the disheartened, and refuge to the emotionally displaced. When he is near, burdensome feelings cannot linger long, so never hesitate to cling to him in times of spiritual distress, when you need to feel God's blessing and encouragement the most.

Haniel's smile just makes my heart melt, and I think it would be quite difficult for a **clairvoyant** or **dreamer** to not feel her burdened heart lighten whenever he makes an appearance. As one of the most graceful angels in Heaven, Haniel's movements are fluid and refined. (I can never get enough of watching him walk with those long, slow strides.) Always quick to make polite gestures, he's quite the gentleman. Visions of him are sure to instill a sense of peace and security, as well as grant a reminder that no matter what you may have done in this lifetime, God's grace is sufficient.

Archangel Iophiel

MEANING OF NAME: *Beauty of God.*

PATRON ANGEL OF: Architects, artists, art historians, art museum curators and benefactors, art teachers, community beautification groups, fashion designers and models, film directors and production crews, gardeners, interior decorators, masons, painters, philanthropists, photographers, sculptors, secrets, visionaries, wedding planners.

ADDITIONAL NAMES/AVATARS: Jofiel, Jophiel, Zophiel.

HEAVENLY ASSIGNMENT: Iophiel opens our eyes to the beauty of God that surrounds us, as well as to the beauty that dwells within the human soul. She is quick to offer encouragement to those with low self-esteem, and inspiration to those in an artistic rut.

USUALLY ARRIVES IN YOUR LIFE: When you need to slow down and make rest, respite, and recreation integral parts of the healing process, whether this healing is of the body, mind, or soul.

PROMOTES/EVOKES: Ambition, bliss, creativeness, delight, giggles, self-esteem.

DIFFUSES: Conceit, embarrassment, failure, meagerness, mediocrity, shyness, feelings of unattractiveness.

ENERGY SIGNATURE (TEMPERATURE/SPEED/ELEMENT): Hot/Rapid/Fire.

ASCENDED MASTERS WITH SIMILAR ENERGY SIGNATURES: Aphrodite, Athena, Guinevere, Lakshmi, Mary Magdalene, Oonagh, Oshun, Vesta.

WINGS: Pearl white.

USUAL ATTIRE: Bright, colorful skirts and tunics. Michael once referred to her as a "walking rainbow."

ICONS: Quarterstaff, roses (all except black and white), swan.

ANIMALS: Bee, bison, cougar/panther, cow, fox, frog, hummingbird, parrot, peacock, seals and sea lions, swan, tiger.

VEGETATION: Alfalfa, allspice, amaranth, apple, apricot, avocado, Brazil nut, cabbage, cardamom, carnation, cherry, cinnamon, corn, daisy, geraniums, gourd, grain, grape, henna, hibiscus, hyacinth, jasmine, licorice, lilac, lime, mistletoe, oat, orange, orchid, pansy, papaya, peach, pear, pimento, pomegranate, primrose, rose, sassafras, strawberry, tomato, vanilla, wheat, yohimbe (poison).

OBJECTS: Art museums, carnivals, festivals, flowers, flower gardens, quarterstaff, rainbows, suncatchers, sunlight.

PLANET: Venus, Saturn.

DAY: Friday.

SEASON: Summer.

BASIC ELEMENT: Fire.

METALS: Brass, copper.

CRYSTALS & GEMSTONES: Agate, chrysoprase, crystal quartz, jade (green, pink), malachite, opal, tourmaline (green, pink), rhodochrosite, rhodonite, rose quartz, ruby.

SHAPES: Curves, rolling hills, semicircle.

CHAKRAS: Sacral, heart.

MUSICAL NOTE: G.

MUSICAL INSTRUMENTS: All.

COLORS: Vibrant, summery colors.

NUMERICAL VIBRATION: 8.

SCENTS: Apple blossom, apricot, carnation, cherry, cinnamon, grape, hyacinth, jasmine, lilac, lime, orange, papaya, peach, pear, pomegranate, rose, strawberry, tuberose, vanilla.

SCENT TYPES: Floral, fruit, scents of hearth and home (fresh baked bread, homemade meals, etc.).

CLOTHING (TEXTILE): Silk.

YOUR PERSONAL ASSOCIATIONS, VISUAL CUES, AND NOTES:

_____

_____

_____

_____

_____

Connecting with Iophiel

Clairsentients best beware of Iophiel, for they will be highly susceptible to the angel's bubbly personality and prone to giggle fits. Expect lively and carefree exchanges with Iophiel that will elevate your spirit and put a beaming smile on your face.

The **clairaudient** will find it very easy to have casual conversations with Iophiel, as this angel never seems to mind talking about daily life in the human realm. Her voice is sugar-sweet, but she tends to talk extremely fast. If you're having trouble understanding her, don't hesitate to ask her to slow down for you.

Clairvoyants and **dreamers** will be wowed by Iophiel's vivaciousness. Often cloaked in a bright array of colors, this angel tends to be very fairylike. Don't be fooled, however—Iophiel can be just as fierce as Archangel Michael in battle. So, don't mistake her girlishness for weakness. She may remind you of Tinker Bell, but she can kick butt like Mulan.

Archangel Metatron

MEANING OF NAME: *Little YHWH* (Little Yahweh).

PATRON ANGEL OF: Accountants, archivists, babysitters, bankers, children, child psychologists, librarians, nannies, pediatricians, sacred geometry, scribes, storytellers, teachers.

ADDITIONAL NAMES/AVATARS: Merraton, Metaraon, Metatetron, Mittron.

HEAVENLY ASSIGNMENT: Metatron loves children and enjoys teaching. He is also delegated the task of keeping heavenly records and is associated with both the Book of Life and the akashic records.

USUALLY ARRIVES IN YOUR LIFE: When you are embarking upon new, uncharted territory in your spiritual journey and are in need of company and security.

PROMOTES/EVOKES: Familial love, nurturing, parental protection, security, wholeness.

DIFFUSES: Foolhardiness, incompetence, reclusiveness, feelings of pointlessness.

ENERGY SIGNATURE (TEMPERATURE/SPEED/ELEMENT): Cool/Slow/Aether.

ASCENDED MASTERS WITH SIMILAR ENERGY SIGNATURES: Devi, Ganesh, Ho Tai, St. Nicholas.

WINGS: Countless rainbow wings.

USUAL ATTIRE: I have never seen Metatron take a human form, and it's said that he rarely shows his wings. He is usually a formless mist of bright white light mingled with prism colors. When I connect with him, he usually holds me in the palm of his hand, which is formed out of clouds and big enough to make me—a big, southern-fed gal—feel like a peapod pixie.

ICONS: Books, clouds, rainbows.

ANIMALS: Ant, crane, elephant, goldfish, goose, kitten, mouse, ostrich, prairie dog, puppy, stork.

VEGETATION: Celery, chamomile, coconut, gotu kola, hemp, lavender, passion flower, poppy, valerian, walnut.

OBJECTS: Books, clouds, grassy fields, institutions of education and banking, libraries, rainbows, sleep.

PLANET: Moon.

DAY: Monday.

SEASON: Fall.

BASIC ELEMENT: Aether.

METALS: Platinum, silver.

CRYSTALS & GEMSTONES: Agate, crystal quartz, dioptase, malachite-azurite, moonstone, topaz.

SHAPES: Enneagram, Metatron's cube, star polygon.

CHAKRAS: Third eye, crown.

MUSICAL NOTE: D.

MUSICAL INSTRUMENTS: Fiddle, voice.

COLORS: All colors.

NUMERICAL VIBRATION: 4.

SCENTS: Coconut, lavender, passion flower.

SCENT TYPES: Light and airy, tropical.

CLOTHING (TEXTILE): "Love and light."

YOUR PERSONAL ASSOCIATIONS, VISUAL CUES, AND NOTES:

_____

_____

_____

_____

_____

_____

Connecting with Metatron

Metatron has a fatherly presence to him, and those connecting with him shouldn't be surprised to find themselves connecting with their inner child when he is around.

Recurring **dreams** or **clairvoyant** visions of a white mist or fog indicate that Metatron is near, and seeking your attention. Because this archangel works more behind the scenes than directly with humans, such dreams are designed more to promote introspection than enable divine connection.

Though I have never seen Metatron's human form, clients and students alike have described him as a very tall, older-looking angel with warm, deep-set eyes. Some said he was bearded, others say he's clean-shaven, but they all agree that his tall stature is not intimidating. If anything, it adds to the air of protection and security that he often exudes.

While **clairaudients** will usually hear their angels' voices in their right ear, Metatron's voice is often in surround sound. Its deep bass gently reverberates through you, easing you into a state of tranquility.

Though Metatron is the tallest angel in Heaven, his presence can be very subtle for **clairsentients**. From a gentle breeze on the cheek to the sensation of a feather-light touch on the arm, Metatron's interactions with clairsentients will come across as soothingly as a mother's touch.

Archangel Michael

MEANING OF NAME: *Who Is As God.*

PATRON ANGEL OF: Auto racing, basketball, body builders, dancers, firemen, football, health and fitness, military, police, protectors of truth and justice, sports and competition, sun and beach worshippers, surfer dudes and dudettes, wrestlers.

ADDITIONAL NAMES/AVATARS: Beshter, Mika'il, Sabbathiel, St. Michael.

HEAVENLY ASSIGNMENT: Michael is the General of Heaven's Armies. And while he's the most beloved angel, he is also the Universal Champion of Wrestling. He's the Terminator of the Universe, kicking butt and taking names across the galaxies.

USUALLY ARRIVES IN YOUR LIFE: When the environment in which you live is about to drastically change, whether it's a change in residence, job/career, or family/friend dynamics.

PROMOTES/EVOKES: Assertiveness, bravery, courage, cunning, freedom, happiness, pride, strength, team spirit, wittiness.

DIFFUSES: Aggression, anger, despair, disappointment, dread, exclusion, hostility, worry.

ENERGY SIGNATURE (TEMPERATURE/SPEED/ELEMENT): Hot/Rapid/Fire.

ASCENDED MASTERS WITH SIMILAR ENERGY SIGNATURES: Apollo, Brighid, Horus, Krishna, Kuan Ti, Odin, Osiris, Pele.

WINGS: White.

USUAL ATTIRE: Wears traditional white angel robes…with the tunic's sleeves torn off to display his broad shoulders and muscular arms. Sometimes he'll rip the tunic off altogether.

ICONS: Eagle, flag, javelin, lion, medieval armor, scales of justice, shield, sword.

ANIMALS: Bear, bull, cardinal, cock, eagle, falcon, hawk, lion.

VEGETATION: Acacia, angelica, ash, banana, bay, black cohosh, black pepper, carrot, cashew, chili pepper, cinnamon, date, fennel, fig, ginseng, nutmeg, olive, onion, patchouli, rose, saffron, sesame, sunflower.

OBJECTS: Beaches, candles, energy, gymnasiums, heat, light, luminaries, medieval armor, sunlight, swimming pools, swords.

PLANETS: Sun, Mars.

DAY: Sunday.

SEASON: Summer.

BASIC ELEMENT: Fire.

METALS: Gold, platinum, titanium.

CRYSTALS & GEMSTONES: Agate, bloodstone, carnelian, cat's eye, crystal quartz, diamond, emerald, garnet, hawk's eye, sunstone.

SHAPES: Triangle, pyramid.

CHAKRAS: Root, sacral, solar plexus, crown.

MUSICAL NOTE: C.

MUSICAL INSTRUMENTS: Electric guitar, piano.

COLORS: Gold, orange, red, white, yellow.

NUMERICAL VIBRATIONS: 1, 3.

SCENTS: Amber, cinnamon, musk, patchouli, tuberose.

SCENT TYPES: Earthy, fiery, spicy, warm musk.

CLOTHING (TEXTILE): None (nude!)

_____

_____

_____

_____

_____

Connecting with Michael

Watch out, **clairsentients**, Michael is hot stuff…literally. Those who connect with this angel through the art of feeling can expect a brief flash of heat that starts in the hips, spirals through the coccyx, and explodes in the small of the back, sending warmth throughout the body. It's a feeling that can leave you winded, but energized and invigorated.

Michael is quite chatty for a guy, so **clairaudients** will find him easy to talk with. His sense of humor and wittiness know no bounds, and those who are blessed enough to hear the voice of Heaven's General can expect to be filled with laughter. There is never a dull moment with him around.

Dreamers or those with **clairvoyant** skills can expect to be dazzled by this most beloved angel in Heaven. His bright eyes and sunny smile can chase away storm clouds and fill your soul with a renewed hope and exuberance. Michael is hardly vain, but he does love to show off and enjoys being seen, so clairvoyants should have little trouble connecting with him. You're definitely in store for a magical treat.

Archangel Raguel

MEANING OF NAME: *Friend of God.*

PATRON ANGEL OF: Agriculture, community organizers, community planners, farmers, industry, land owners, managers (supervisors, foremen, etc.), manual laborers, multitaskers.

ADDITIONAL NAMES/AVATARS: Akrasiel, Rufael, Raguil, Rasuil, Suryan.

HEAVENLY ASSIGNMENT: Raguel is like a department manager who receives work orders from the Heavenly Throne and then distributes them among the archangels. He's a high-octane, laser-focused individual. Archangel Michael says Raguel moves so fast that sometimes the angels cannot even see him.

USUALLY ARRIVES IN YOUR LIFE: When it's time to reorganize your priorities and get down to business.

PROMOTES/EVOKES: Ambition, application, humility, longevity, selflessness, solidarity, stamina, tenacity.

DIFFUSES: Idleness, indecisiveness, ineffectiveness, inefficiency, laziness, procrastination.

ENERGY SIGNATURE (TEMPERATURE/SPEED/ELEMENT): Varies/Rapid/Air.

ASCENDED MASTERS WITH SIMILAR ENERGY SIGNATURES: Lu-Hsing, Moses, Solomon.

WINGS: Royal blue.

USUAL ATTIRE: Raguel usually wears flowing robes of different shades of blue, but has been known to wear academic regalia (sans the cap) that make him look like a college professor at a graduation ceremony.

ICONS: Books, quill and ink.

ANIMALS: Antelope, beasts of burden, mouse, roadrunner, swift.

VEGETATION: Bean, hickory, lucky hand (orchid family), marigold, pecan, straw, yerba mate.

OBJECTS: Agriculture, books, energy, fruit trees and orchards, heat, industry, quill and ink, small communities, vegetable gardens.

PLANETS: Mercury, Uranus.

DAY: Wednesday.

SEASON: Fall.

BASIC ELEMENT: Air.

METAL: Mercury (poison).

CRYSTALS & GEMSTONES: Agate, amazonite, chrysocolla, crystal quartz, gold calcite, onyx, smoky quartz, tiger's eye.

SHAPES: Squares, 90-degree angles.

CHAKRAS: Root, throat.

MUSICAL NOTE: B.

MUSICAL INSTRUMENT: Lyre.

COLORS: All shades of blue.

NUMERICAL VIBRATION: 2.

SCENT: Hickory.

SCENT TYPES: Woodsy, smoky.

CLOTHING (TEXTILE): Denim.

YOUR PERSONAL ASSOCIATIONS, VISUAL CUES, AND NOTES:

_____

_____

_____

_____

_____

Connecting with Raguel

No matter what type of connection you prefer to use, interactions with the Department Manager of Heaven will often be brief.

Unfortunately for the **clairvoyants**, Raguel may be hard to see. This archangel seems to move at the speed of light, slowing down for no one. Connecting with Raguel this way, without drawing on clairaudience as well, may prove challenging because you won't be able to make him stop to communicate his message. Because of that, I encourage clairvoyants to work with signs when engaging this angel. That, or try to finagle him into giving you his email address. (Good luck with that.)

Clairsentients will feel abuzz with energy as they connect with Raguel. It's almost like lying on a vibrating bed, only instead of feeling relaxed, you feel motivated to be productive and get things done. After connecting with him, don't be surprised to find yourself full of energy and the desire to spring clean or alphabetize your CD collection.

Clairaudients will find Raguel's tone to be direct and concise. This angel economizes time and words, and will rarely engage in idle chitchat. That said, approach him like you would an accountant or lawyer—be fully prepared and ready to work.

A long while back, when I was launching a new business venture, I found myself panicking because I wasn't familiar with contract law; the contract I was slammed with required an expert lawyer. I was on a tight budget (of $0) and couldn't afford any counsel. After biting my nails for a few weeks and realizing that I hadn't a clue what to do with the contract, I called up a good friend for a shoulder to cry on.

Her response: "There has to be an angel in Heaven who knows about business law."

"Oh, yeah!" The light bulb clicked on. I hung up the phone, and before I could utter the last syllable of his name, the angel appeared before me.

"Yes?" Raguel arched a brow and folded his arms.

"Help?" I squeaked, clutching the contract. In my mind's eye, I saw the angel manifest his own copy of the contract and immediately begin to leaf through the pages.

"Get rid of this..." he began, "and this. Ask for more here, and make them specify what they mean here. This clause is way too broad."

The angel's presence made my head spin, and I could barely keep up with him as I scribbled down notes. He then instructed me to amend the contract with something I knew the other party would object to.

Blinking in confusion, I looked up to the angel. "There's no way they'll agree to that, Raguel."

The angel gave me an indignant glare. "Chantel, do you want my help or not?"

"Yeah, but…" I whimpered.

"Well, you just got it. Make the changes and send it back." He disappeared before I could even thank him.

Doubtful but undaunted, I followed his instructions to the letter, and after a few agonizing weeks of silence, the other party contacted me.

They were willing to fully agree with the new terms.

So while Raguel may come across as abrasive sometimes, his guidance is invaluable and you don't even have to pay him by the hour.

That said, always remember that the angels will tell us what we need to hear to propel us forward through God's Great Equation. Raguel's changes could have very well led to disaster, but that wasn't meant to be. If the contract, and therefore the venture, fell through, then that was all part of the plan to begin with. Would I be steamed at Raguel for playing a part in that, if the contract changes had resulted in a debacle? Heck, yes. I'm *still* sore at Gabriel for landing me in a hospital years ago, but I understand that everything happens according to divine timing. The angels are here primarily to execute God's orders, and secondly to guide us through.

Archangel Ramiel

MEANING OF NAME: *God's Mercy.*

PATRON ANGEL OF: Archeologists, archivists, economic analysts, educators, family elders, forensic specialists, historians, history museum curators, librarians, prophets, shamans, statisticians, stenographers, stock markets, tribal elders.

ADDITIONAL NAMES/AVATARS: Jermiel, Phanuel, Remiel, Yerahmeel. (Has been often interchanged with Uriel in historical and religious texts.)

HEAVENLY ASSIGNMENT: Ramiel maintains the chronicles of both Heaven and Earth.

USUALLY ARRIVES IN YOUR LIFE: When it's time to revisit your past and recognize your life's patterns in order to facilitate future healing and growth.

PROMOTES/EVOKES: Accuracy, curiosity, patience, punctuality.

DIFFUSES: Aimlessness, confusion, limbo, wandering.

ENERGY SIGNATURE (TEMPERATURE/SPEED/ELEMENT): Cold/Slow/Earth.

ASCENDED MASTERS WITH SIMILAR ENERGY SIGNATURES: Chronos, Janus, Father Time/Baby New Year, Noah, Seshat.

WINGS: White, but rarely displays them.

USUAL ATTIRE: Ramiel's attire has always reminded me of a Catholic monk; he sports brown wool robes with a simple rope around his waist.

ICONS: Calendar, hourglass, sundial.

ANIMALS: Owl, squirrel, wood rat.

VEGETATION: Ivy, papyrus, pecan, vanilla, walnut.

OBJECTS: Any device that measures time (calendars, clocks), any instrument that aids in historical research and documentation (books, files), museums, paper (papyrus, parchment, rice), rocks, soil, time capsules, writing instruments.

PLANET: Jupiter.

DAY: Thursday.

SEASON(S): All seasons.

BASIC ELEMENT: Earth.

METALS: Copper, tin.

CRYSTALS & GEMSTONES: Agate, alexandrite, cat's eye, crystal quartz, sodalite.

SHAPES: Abstract.

CHAKRA: Solar plexus.

MUSICAL NOTE: B.

MUSICAL INSTRUMENTS: Bells, violin.

COLORS: Earth tones.

NUMERICAL VIBRATIONS: 2, 5.

SCENT: Vanilla.

SCENT TYPE: Sweet.

CLOTHING (TEXTILE): Cotton, wool.

YOUR PERSONAL ASSOCIATIONS, VISUAL CUES, AND NOTES:

_____

_____

_____

_____

_____

_____

Connecting with Ramiel

Those who are fortunate enough to connect with Ramiel through sleep may find themselves in a state of lucid **dreaming** from time to time. Lucid dreaming occurs when the dreamer is fully aware that she is dreaming—upon realizing this, she can sometimes control her dreamworld and manipulate it in ways she sees fit. No doubt Ramiel has a hand in cocrafting this dreamscape, in order to better share his insight about theories of time or multiple realities/dimensions. These spiritual concepts are difficult to explore through mundane study, and instead require immersion and firsthand experience.

Other than his involvement with dreams, Ramiel is a shy angel and prefers observing humans rather than interacting with them. If you do happen to encounter him in a meditation, you can expect him to take you through a review of your past—be it of this lifetime or a past life.

Because he works behind the scenes, **clairaudients**, **clairsentients**, and **clairvoyants** might not connect with Ramiel directly, but instead receive faint intuitive clues—guidance by way of quiet inspiration. Ramiel's influence is so subtle that you may not even realize he's near.

Archangel Raphael

Meaning of Name: *God Heals.*

Patron Angel of: Astronomers, cartographers, doctors, healers, herbalists, intuitives, light workers (acupuncturists, chiropractors, kinesiologists, massage therapists, Reiki practitioners, yogis, etc.), the medical field, nurses, shamans and medicine women, stargazers, travelers.

Additional Names/Avatars: None.

Heavenly assignment: To teach and bestow the gifts of healing, intuition, and wisdom.

Usually arrives in your life: When healing or a significant transition is afoot.

Promotes/Evokes: Awe, compassion, curiosity, discovery, empathy, introspection, stillness, sympathy, wholeness, wonder.

Diffuses: Confusion, feelings of frailty, misery, suffering, worry.

Energy Signature (Temperature/Speed/Element): Cold/Slow/Water.

Ascended Masters with Similar Energy Signatures: Ishtar, Isis, Khonsu, Merlin, Neptune, St. Padre Pio.

Wings: White, but rarely displays them.

Usual Attire: Like Gabriel, Raphael usually wears white, billowing robes. But when this archangel of healing is meandering about in his castle tower, he'll wear robes of purple, blue, and gold.

ICONS: Dolphin, mortar and pestle, shepherd's crook, white dove.

ANIMALS: Aquatic life, cat (domestic), deer, dolphin, dove (white), dragonfly, duck, frog, horse, owl, rabbit, snake, whale, wolf.

VEGETATION: African violet, aloe, barley, blackberry, carob, catnip, chamomile, dill, echinacea, elm, eucalyptus, eyebright, flax, frankincense, golden seal, kelp, lavender, mandrake, marigold, mesquite, moss, myrrh, oregano, parsley, plum, potato, sage, seaweed, spearmint, St. John's wort, star anise, tea, thyme, turmeric, willow, yarrow, yucca.

OBJECTS: Air travel, algae, boats and ships, constellations, dreamscape, elves, enchanted forests, fairies, imagination, marinas, mortar and pestle, mountains, oceans and seas, outer space, planets, plasma (charged particles), shadows, shepherd's crook, unicorn.

PLANET: Mercury.

DAY: Wednesday.

SEASON: Winter.

BASIC ELEMENT: Water.

METAL: Silver.

CRYSTALS & GEMSTONES: Agate, amethyst, ametrine, aquamarine, aventurine (blue, green), crystal quartz, emerald, lapis lazuli, sugilite, turquoise.

SHAPES: Spirals.

CHAKRAS: Third eye, crown.

MUSICAL NOTE: E.

MUSICAL INSTRUMENTS: Flute, voice (especially the voices of the fairies).

COLORS: Black, blue, deep reds, gold, green, purple, silver, turquoise.

NUMERICAL VIBRATION: 6.

SCENTS: Ambergris, eucalyptus, frankincense and myrrh, lavender, sage, spearmint.

SCENT TYPES: Exotic; oceans and seas.

CLOTHING (TEXTILE): Wool.

YOUR PERSONAL ASSOCIATIONS, VISUAL CUES, AND NOTES:

_____

_____

_____

_____

_____

_____

Connecting with Raphael

Like Cassiel, Archangel Raphael enjoys connecting with us through dreamscape. Since he is an angel who sparks the imagination like no other, **dreamers** can expect vivid visions that will be difficult to forget. Raphael's dreams are often peaceful, but also loads of fun—he can craft magical dreamworlds that dazzle, enchant, and inspire. The same can be said of the meditative reality he creates, for anyone who connects with him through meditation or **clairvoyance**.

To the **clairaudient**, Raphael's voice is very soft, almost a whisper. His tone is unimposing, as he never tells you what you *must* do (unlike Gabriel or Raguel). Instead, he merely offers suggestions for you to ponder. Connecting with him is much like having a heart-to-heart talk with a loving, protective father.

The **clairsentient** will instantly feel safe and secure under the watchful eye of this gentle giant. When he draws near, turbulent emotions are quelled and hope is renewed. Raphael is the Angel of Healing, and clairsentients will be quick to sense his soothing energies as they radiate in your heart center, behind your eyes, or at the center of your brow.

Archangel Raziel

MEANING OF NAME: *Secret of God.*

PATRON ANGEL OF: Alchemy, computer science, cryptography, linguists, mathematics, metaphysics, mysteries, prophets, sacred geometry, scholars, secrets, the unknown, visionaries.

ADDITIONAL NAMES/AVATARS: Angel of Mysteries, Akrasiel, Gallizur, Ratziel, Saraqael, Suriel.

HEAVENLY ASSIGNMENT: His name says it all. Archangel Raziel is the keeper of Heaven's most classified information. According to historical texts, he knows things that no other angel knows and is entrusted by God to be a fortified vault of the universe's deepest mysteries.

USUALLY ARRIVES IN YOUR LIFE: For the most part, Raziel is a hands-off angel and prefers to work in the background rather than in the foreground of someone's life. But those connecting with him do so at a time when a revelation is to be imparted that will help further their spiritual growth.

PROMOTES/EVOKES: Catharsis, curiosity, dedication, discipline, discovery, epiphany, loyalty, quietude, reticence, stealth, wisdom.

DIFFUSES: Aggravation, belligerence, deceit, dissent, gossip, ignorance, mutiny, suspicion.

ENERGY SIGNATURE (TEMPERATURE/SPEED/ELEMENT): Cold/Slow/Aether.

ASCENDED MASTERS WITH SIMILAR ENERGY SIGNATURES: None. At least, none that he's divulging at the moment.

WINGS: Black and gray with strands of silver.

USUAL ATTIRE: If ever there was an angel who knew how to blend in with the shadows, Raziel would be the one. A chameleon of sorts, he's an expert at stealth and often goes completely undetected by humans and angels alike. He often dresses in dark colors, if not all black, but dons white formal robes while standing before the Throne. Otherwise, sporting black denim or leather, he can rival Cassiel when it comes to looking like some roguish antihero from a comic book.

ICONS: Blade/dagger, illuminated mind, keys, smoke (mist), veil.

ANIMALS: Chameleon, eel, fox, panther, raven, scorpion, snake, spider.

VEGETATION: Belladonna (poison), eyebright, garlic, hemlock (poison), hickory.

OBJECTS: Camouflage, cloaks, codes, diaries, glyphs, hoods/cowls, information, keys, locks, matrices, nighttime, shadows, smoke, vaults, veils.

PLANET: Neptune.

DAY: Wednesday.

SEASON: Winter.

BASIC ELEMENT: Aether.

METAL: Mercury, titanium.

CRYSTALS & GEMSTONES: Diamond, hematite, jet, obsidian, smoky quartz.

SHAPES: Labyrinth, maze.

CHAKRAS: Third eye, crown.

MUSICAL NOTE: B.

MUSICAL INSTRUMENTS: Chimes.

COLORS: Black, gray, navy, dark red.

NUMERICAL VIBRATION: 0.

SCENTS: Hickory.

SCENT TYPES: Woodsy, smoky.

CLOTHING (TEXTILE): Leather.

YOUR PERSONAL ASSOCIATIONS, VISUAL CUES, AND NOTES:

_____

_____

_____

Connecting with Raziel

If you find yourself dreaming about a cloaked, enigmatic figure, it's time to begin some serious dream journaling. Archangel Raziel lurks in the **dreamscape**, imparting bits of wisdom and glimpses of the esoteric. Whether it's through dreams or **clairvoyant** visions, you can expect Raziel's messages to be as cryptic as the archangel delivering them. Dutifully recording the signs and symbols he provides, along with some old-fashioned sleuthing (either on the Internet or in the library), will eventually lead you to profound discoveries about the angel, yourself, and perhaps even the realm of spirit.

Archangel Raziel is an angel of few words, and even the few words he shares will reveal little to nothing. Yet I enjoy talking with Raziel. He's secretive, but not entirely antisocial. With a knowing grin, he's come back at me with quite a few quips, especially while I was working on this book. When it was his turn to be interviewed, he stood before me with his arms folded, leaning back against his motorbike and peering at me with eyes so light blue they were almost translucent.

"You're going to make this hard on me, aren't you?" I peered at him over my laptop screen as his lips slowly creased into a sinister grin.

"You know, I really should, just to make you miserable." His voice was low, his scrutinizing eyes narrowing on me. "You knew darn well we needed to do this weeks ago, but yet again, you wait until the last minute." My contrite gaze lowered to my fingers, arched over my keyboard. I was at a loss for words, really. After all, he was right. I was procrastinating on the project like I always do.

"But if you don't help me, then the book won't be completed and I don't think Raphael will like that," I whined.

"Which is why I'm willing to talk … this time. What do you want to know?" He flashed a soft smile and didn't seem to hold out on too much information.

But for more serious work, like prophecy, metaphysics, and the arcane, **clairaudients** shouldn't expect Raziel to be so liberal. Subtle whispers and intuitive insight is more his *modus operandi*.

The archangel's presence is chilly, but not uncomfortable. **Clairsentients** may notice a subtle drop in room temperature or feel a chill tingle on their skin. Beyond Raziel's energy signature, his presence has a very unique feeling of heaviness. The air seems denser when he's around—if he wants to be detected. Clairsentients may feel a bit fatigued or sedated when connecting with him, so it's best to engage this angel in your sacred space, where you feel comfortable and don't have to focus on being alert or fully aware of your surroundings.

Archangel Sandalphon

MEANING OF NAME: *Brother.*

PATRON ANGEL OF: Academics, children with disabilities, concentration, florists, gifts and charity, the homeless, law, mathematics, midwives, music, playfulness and games (board games, video games), prayer, puzzles, riddles, secrets, school exams, unborn children, youth.

ADDITIONAL NAMES/AVATARS: Elijah the Prophet, Ophan, Sandolfon.

HEAVENLY ASSIGNMENT: To calm, uplift, or enlighten souls through the use of music and the imagination. He is Heaven's Chief Muse.

USUALLY ARRIVES IN YOUR LIFE: When you need to find common ground between work and play. Not all work has to be arduous, and not all play is merely a way to pass the time. To discover the middle ground between the two is to discover a life of perfect harmony.

PROMOTES/EVOKES: Affection, cheer, cleverness, concentration, curiosity, devotion, generosity, giddiness, gratitude, harmony, humility, love, playfulness.

DIFFUSES: Boredom, depression, grumpiness, jealousy, loneliness, nervousness, feelings of abandonment.

ENERGY SIGNATURE (TEMPERATURE/SPEED/ELEMENT): Warm/Even/Aether.

ASCENDED MASTERS WITH SIMILAR ENERGY SIGNATURES: Cherubs, Cupid, Damara, elves and fairies, Hathor, John the Baptist, Kwan Yin, St. Theresa.

WINGS: Beige and brown, but rarely displays them.

USUAL ATTIRE: Sandalphon prefers a simple pair of brown trousers, a white-collared shirt with the sleeves rolled up, suspenders, and a pair of comfortable loafers.

When in his formal attire, he dons traditional white robes and prefers to wear sandals or go barefoot.

ICONS: Baseball and children's games, candy, celebrations, harp, wrapped presents.

ANIMALS: Canary, coyote, dog, otter, porcupine.

VEGETATION: Blueberry, daffodil, gardenia, grass, honeysuckle, lemon, lemon balm, lemongrass, lettuce, magnolia, moss, passion flower, pineapple, raspberry, rhubarb, strawberry, sugarcane, sweet pea, tulip, violet.

OBJECTS: Amusement parks, barbershops, barbershop quartets, baseball, bubblegum, candy, classrooms, comic books, games (board, children's, video), gifts, grassy fields, laughter, mashed potatoes, miniature golf, pancakes (and syrup!), playgrounds, pleasant surprises, secret passageways, school buildings, wild flowers, wrapped presents.

PLANET: Venus.

DAY: Friday.

SEASON: Spring.

BASIC ELEMENT: Aether.

METAL: Copper.

CRYSTALS & GEMSTONES: Agate, blue tourmaline, crystal quartz, fluorite.

SHAPES: Gentle waves, Cuisenaire rods.

CHAKRAS: Sacral, heart.

MUSICAL NOTE: G.

MUSICAL INSTRUMENTS: All instruments, especially together in a symphony orchestra or music band.

COLORS: Bright happy colors; browns and blues.

NUMERICAL VIBRATION: 7.

SCENTS: Citrus, blueberry, gardenia, grassy fields, pineapple, strawberry, sweet pea.

SCENT TYPES: Floral, sweet scents of the hearth and home (cakes and pies, etc.).

CLOTHING (TEXTILE): Cotton.

YOUR PERSONAL ASSOCIATIONS, VISUAL CUES, AND NOTES:

_____

_____

_____

_____

_____

_____

Connecting with Sandalphon

Clairaudients will have their ears serenaded by the most melodious voice in Heaven. Playful yet soft-spoken, this archangel enjoys fun and casual conversation. He's a wonderful angel for beginner clairaudients to work with, even if he's not your mentoring angel. Expect his words to be loving and cheerful … unless Michael is around. At that point, you can expect to hear the duo banter like Abbott and Costello. There's something about Michael that brings out the slightly naughty side of Sandalphon's childlike nature. The warrior angel definitely has an influence on his kid brother.

Expect your heart to go pitter-patter if you connect with Sandalphon through **clairsentience**. This angel was one of the spiritual influences for the Roman god Cupid, so feelings of elation and *everything is right with the world* are not uncommon when encountering him. As with Iophiel, clairsentients can expect a case of the giggles with Sandalphon; he is a master tummy-tickler.

"But I'm not ticklish," you might say. To which I reply, "Everyone has a ticklish spot, and Sandalphon *will* find it." As Heaven's Peter Pan, he enjoys connecting with humans to draw out their inner child.

This bright and chirpy angel is a perfect picture of youth and vitality. While the benevolent hosts of Heaven all surpass any and every human notion of beauty, I find Sandalphon's beauty to be unrivaled. (I'm sure Michael would playfully disagree.) Beginner **clairvoyants** may find it difficult to pull away from visions of Sandalphon, as his radiance will lure you in and hold you captive until his messages of compassion, charity, and love take root.

Because of this, **dreamers** will find themselves whimpering in protest as a dream ends and they're pulled back into the waking world. (My alarm clock met a violent demise when it woke me out of a dream with Sandalphon one morning.)

Archangel Uriel

MEANING OF NAME: *Fire of God.*

PATRON ANGEL OF: Judges, lawmakers, peacemakers, prophets, seekers of truth, upholders of justice, visionaries.

ADDITIONAL NAMES/AVATARS: Israfel, Jehoel, Jeremiel, Nuriel, Paruel, Phanuel, Prince of Lights, Regent of the Sun, Suriel, Urjan, Uryan, Vretil.

HEAVENLY ASSIGNMENT: Assigned to bring all sentient beings before the Throne of God on the Day of Reckoning.

USUALLY ARRIVES IN YOUR LIFE: In all my years of consulting, I can probably count on one hand the times I've seen Uriel with a client. Encounters with him are rare and deeply serious in nature, usually involving someone's path as a scholar or prophet.

PROMOTES/EVOKES: Aggression,† balance, bravery, dread,† fairness, nobility, passion (for a cause), repentance, rectitude.

DIFFUSES: Arrogance, contempt, demoralization, envy, greed, hate, inadequacy, shame, subjugation, weakness.

---

† Uriel is one of the most intense archangels I've ever encountered, so if you're not familiar with him he may seem aggressive and instill a slight sense of fear and unease. Keep in mind that since he is an archangel who reins in the unruly, severity comes with the territory.

ENERGY SIGNATURE (TEMPERATURE/SPEED/ELEMENT): Hot/Rapid/Fire.

ASCENDED MASTERS WITH SIMILAR ENERGY SIGNATURES: Forseti, Idaten, Lilith, Maat, Thor, Thoth.

WINGS: Crimson and gold.

USUAL ATTIRE: Uriel's casual attire is usually a crimson tunic with crimson leather breeches and matching boots. When in his formal attire, he prefers armor of the same color with elaborate gold detailing.

ICONS: Bow and arrow, bullwhip made of flames, chariot, scales of justice.

ANIMALS: Boar, lizard, phoenix, ram, rhinoceros, snow leopard.

VEGETATION: Ash, basil, birch, black pepper, bloodroot, cactus, chili pepper, cinnamon, clove, cumin, curry, fig, garlic, hops, horseradish, juniper, leek, mistletoe, nettle, nutmeg, peppermint, radish, rosemary, sandalwood, shallot, snapdragon, Solomon's seal, thistle, Venus flytrap, wormwood (poison).

OBJECTS: Bow and arrow, bullwhip, chariot, earthquakes, fire and brimstone, floods, molten lava, lightning, scales of justice, thunder, void, volcanoes.

PLANET: Mars.

DAY: Tuesday.

SEASONS: All seasons.

BASIC ELEMENT: Fire.

METALS: Bronze, iron, gold.

CRYSTALS & GEMSTONES: Agate, apache tears, crystal quartz, jet, obsidian, pumice.

SHAPES: Sharp, spiky.

CHAKRAS: Root, solar plexus, third eye.

MUSICAL NOTE: F.

MUSICAL INSTRUMENTS: Marching feet, war drums.

COLORS: Gold, orange, red, yellow.

NUMERICAL VIBRATION: 9.

SCENTS: Cinnamon, nutmeg, sandalwood.

SCENT TYPES: Fiery, pungent, spicy.

CLOTHING (TEXTILE): Armor, leather.

YOUR PERSONAL ASSOCIATIONS, VISUAL CUES, AND NOTES:

_____

_____

_____

_____

_____

_____

Connecting with Uriel

If there is one word that describes Uriel, it's "intense."

This archangel of prophecy, justice, and retribution rarely interacts directly with humans. But if you're one of the chosen few who get to connect with him, you will have little difficulty doing so, no matter what method you select.

Uriel is a no-nonsense angel, so **clairaudients** shouldn't expect him to be much of a conversationalist. Communication with him is simple: he talks, you listen. Furthermore, you had better take notes, because Uriel does not make a habit of repeating himself. This may sound quite severe for an angel, but if you couldn't handle it, he wouldn't have been appointed to you.

Clairsentients may sometimes feel like they're being scrutinized when Uriel is near, but it's only because he demands discipline from those he connects with. He is the teacher of scholars and prophets and teaches by example, requiring them to approach their work and life's journey with all the seriousness and depth that he approaches his own. There is no room in Uriel's book for ego, and he keeps us in check by pinching at our conscience whenever we refuse to be honest with ourselves and others.

Clairvoyants will get an eyeful when dealing with this strong, towering, fiery, and fiercely beautiful angel. Visions or **dreams** of Uriel can be intimidating, but they can be incredibly empowering as well. To know that such a warrior is guiding our every step, cherishing us as he would his own brethren, can bolster our courage and reaffirm our identity as children of God.

Don't be surprised if Uriel frequently changes his appearance. It is merely his way of calibrating your vision so that it can pierce through his human form to see his natural, angelic form—radiant gold and white light. (At the core, all sentient beings look like formless bodies of light; the angels take on human form so as not to frighten those of us who don't have much experience with them.)

Uriel bestows keen vision, which enables clairvoyants to discern one heavenly host from another. Those fortified by his tutelage will be able to recognize an angel's true form without having to rely on icons. In other words, he endows clairvoyants with the ability to see the realm of spirit as it truly exists, without the frontage the angels erect to help make us feel more comfortable with the notion of divinity.

Archangel Zadkiel

MEANING OF NAME: *Righteousness of God.*

PATRON ANGEL OF: Academics, charity groups, ministers, philanthropists, places of worship, prisoners, sacrifice, saints, students.

ADDITIONAL NAMES/AVATARS: Tzadkiel, Zadakiel, Zedekiel, Zidekiel.

HEAVENLY ASSIGNMENT: Archangel Zadkiel connects with the human world to teach compassion and understanding while bestowing blessings of mercy and salvation.

USUALLY ARRIVES IN YOUR LIFE: The ever-benevolent and gentle Zadkiel appears when we need to reexamine our lives and focus on forgiving ourselves and others, as well as adopting a more empathetic and compassionate spirit.

PROMOTES/EVOKES: Acceptance, altruism, courage, forgiveness, generosity, mercy, moderation, selflessness, tolerance.

DIFFUSES: Abrasiveness, angst, apathy, cynicism, egocentricity, extremism, harshness, hostility, selfishness.

ENERGY SIGNATURE (TEMPERATURE/SPEED/ELEMENT): Cool/Even/Earth.

ASCENDED MASTERS WITH SIMILAR ENERGY SIGNATURES: Manjusri, Melchizdek, Nabu.

WINGS: Beige and white.

USUAL ATTIRE: Archangel Zadkiel likes to keep things simple. Either white or brown robes drape his tall frame.

ICONS: Books, dove, scroll, shepherd's crook.

ANIMALS: Beasts of burden, dove, goat, sheep.

VEGETATION: Gourd, olive, peach, pecan, rosemary, oak.

OBJECTS: Intellect, memory.

PLANET: Jupiter.

DAY: Thursday.

SEASONS: Spring.

BASIC ELEMENT: Earth.

METALS: Bronze, copper, iron.

CRYSTALS & GEMSTONES: Amethyst, crystal quartz, jade, kunzite.

SHAPES: Chalice, cup.

CHAKRA: Third eye.

MUSICAL NOTE: D.

MUSICAL INSTRUMENTS: Sounds of nature, choirs.

COLORS: Blues, browns, greens, white.

NUMERICAL VIBRATION: 7.

SCENTS: Earth, peach, rosemary.

SCENT TYPES: Earthy, soft (sweet) floral.

CLOTHING (TEXTILE): Wool.

YOUR PERSONAL ASSOCIATIONS, VISUAL CUES, AND NOTES:

_____

_____

_____

_____

_____

_____

Connecting with Zadkiel

Those connecting with Zadkiel will find meditating, concentration, and mental work a breeze if they allow themselves to relax and bask in the angel's tranquil energies.

Clairaudients can look forward to quiet, reflective exchanges with Archangel Zadkiel. He excels at mentoring, and keeps his instruction simple and straightforward. Zadkiel's voice is deep and commanding, but hardly intimidating. Much like Metatron, he has a fatherly presence; those connecting with him will find conversations to be casual and engaging.

When Zadkiel first appeared to me, I was a bit surprised to find that he seemed to be a bit older than the other angels I've connected with. For the most part, Michael and company all look to be in their early thirties (with the exceptions of Sandalphon and Ariel, who look like they're in their teens). But Zadkiel appeared to be a bit older, with flowing gray hair and a groomed gray beard. Make no mistake, though—he still looked fit, and capable of doing damage on the battlefield should Michael call him to the front lines.

Of course, this archangel of mercy can assume a different form for **clairvoyants** and **dreamers**, but regardless of how he appears, his air of protective strength is unmistakable.

Clairsentients will immediately sense security and peace whenever Zadkiel is near. His presence calms the atmosphere while rejuvenating the spirit as well as the mind.

4

SETTING THE FOUNDATION

As you experiment with the various methods of connecting with the angels described in chapter 2, you should also be focusing on creating an environment in which to do this. As I teach students in my Reiki classes, creating a sacred space in which to practice Reiki (on yourself or on a client) is just as important as practicing the art of Reiki itself. The same goes for connecting with the angels, especially for beginners. Later on, once you've engaged the angels a lot and have honed your personal method of connection, you'll become aware of the sacred space you carry *within* you every day—a human's internal temple, so to speak—which you can visit anytime, regardless of what's around you. Until then, however, I consider creating a special place, where you can go to commune with your Creator and guides, to be an important first step on this spiritual journey.

Creating Your Sacred Space

Your sacred space is a place that *you* deem hallowed—a place where you can go when you need to rest your mind, body, and soul. The point of creating a sacred space is to have a spot where you can step outside of your mundane world without having to worry about distractions. With this in mind, ask yourself how much space you can spare. Can you convert a walk-in closet, or can you use a corner of the bedroom? Is this space secluded, and away from heavy "psychic traffic" such as televisions, radios, telephones, people, etc.?

When creating your sacred space, you must do so with love, joy, and peace in your heart. If creating your sacred space is stressful because you wanted brick-red paint for your room's borders instead of sienna, then stop. You don't want to infuse your space with frustration. Take a break and come back to the project with a renewed spirit and an open mind. Furthermore, you don't have to break the bank to create a sacred space in your home (though many of my clients have tried to prove me wrong). Your sacred space can be just a chair facing a blank wall or a chair out in the middle of a spacious garden. What you choose is up to you—but know that it's the purpose and intent that makes the space what it is, not its décor.

Yet for those of you who just must shop at Pier One, let me give you a few pointers. Once you have an idea of how you're going to set up your sacred space, you can have the very fun task of putting it together. Just keep in mind that once you create that space, it should not be used for anything else—this is not a place where you talk on the phone or fold your laundry. I believe that bringing these types of energy into a space intended for solace, stillness, and quietude is counterproductive. The area wouldn't be very good for meditating at that point.

So, you've cleared out a corner of your room, set up a small corner table with a comfortable chair or a zafu, and are now a bit baffled when it comes to finding focus points (objects) that can hold your attention for twenty, forty, sixty minutes at a time (eventually, you will be able to close your eyes and meditate inwardly, without such focus points). I have found that people tend to lean toward bringing the essence of a church or places of worship into their sacred space. Some use candles and incense. Some use bells or singing bowls. Others have statues or photographs.

A quick note on statues: there are many religions that do not tolerate religious icons being displayed in the home (fundamentalist Christianity rejects imagery, and many Islamic traditions prohibit depictions of Allah or the major prophets). In such faiths, statues are considered idolatry. Let me shed a bit of light on that. As someone who has a background in Christianity, the natural arts, and Buddhism, as well as having studied comparative religion my entire life, I do not look at statues as sacred objects. Do I genuflect before an image of Buddha or cross myself as Catholics do before a statue of Mary? Yes. But this is not done in honor of a piece of clay or bronze. This is done in honor of that ascended master and his or her essence, which flows through me.

When I look at my statue of Ganesh, a Hindu deity, I am reminded of his compassion and love for life. When I'm reminded of that, I say to myself, "I want to reflect that same compassion and love for life throughout my reality." When I look at the statue, I respect the Universal Spirit as it manifests in all its different shapes and colors, helping me to elevate my life condition. In Ganesh I see that there are no obstacles between myself and my spiritual growth. In Kwan Yin, I see a loving mother who heeds the cries of the afflicted. In Buddha, I see myself in quiet contemplation, reflecting upon the oneness of myself and Creation. In Jesus, I see my Father, who has nurtured, loved, and taught me everything I know so far. Yes, all these images and more are on my altar, all reflecting what I continually aspire to be—and yet reminding me that, in a way, I'm already that to which I aspire.

But I also understand that they are made of mere clay, and hold no significance beyond that.

So, with all that said, if having a statue of Mother Mary, or an angel, or the wild and untamable Hawaiian volcano goddess Pele helps you to reflect upon your life's aspirations, I see no issue whatsoever with placing it in your sacred space. The one thing you want to be mindful of, at that point, is ensuring that doing so will not cause tension between you and others with whom you may share your living space. Remember, our goal is to bring as much harmony and peace into our lives as possible. Follow the path of compassion, and be willing to compromise on this issue if you must.

In the pages that follow, I discuss various objects that you might like to bring into your sacred space. Follow your intuition! You are the one who will know what works best for you.

Crystals and Gemstones

Crystals and gemstones have been valued for their spiritual and healing properties for thousands of years. Wise men and women with the ability to discern a stone's vibration have used stones for various reasons throughout the ages. Although they may seem rigid and lifeless, stones actually pulsate with vibrations given to them by Mother Earth. They truly are the children of the earth, created deep beneath the soil and forged by heat, pressure, and time. Crystals and gemstones are wonderful conductors of spiritual energy, and I believe that they can assist anyone seeking to hone his or her ability to connect. They make a wonderful addition to a sacred space.

Keep in mind that there is nothing New Age about crystals and gemstones. After all, when God gave Moses the Ten Commandments, he didn't etch them in a tree, scribble them on papyrus, or write them in sand or among the clouds—he wrote them upon stone. To me, stone represents timelessness and the ability to weather anything. It represents strength, endurance, and longevity. It also represents, to me, a firm spiritual foundation. Two thousand years ago, a Jewish prophet said to his disciples, "and upon this rock I will build my church; and the gates of hell shall not prevail against it" (Matthew 16:18). That prophet's church is still standing today.

So, whether you are building a temple or a spiritual practice, the use of stones can be quite beneficial. You will find, below, a brief list of some popular stones, along with a bit of folklore regarding their vibrations and uses. (Note that I do not mention any angel rulerships with the stones here, because this section is about creating your sacred space and infusing it with the harmonizing energy of stones and crystals—it's not about using stones to attract the angels or perform any rituals. Also, I'd like to point out that we're not conducting Wicca or pagan magick here; we're just exploring our natural intuitive abilities.)

Those of you who gravitate toward clairsentience may especially enjoy having stones in your sacred space because of the tangible energies they provide. They're awesome to practice with, and can help potential clairsentients get used to feeling and recognizing different stone vibrations.

Note: The healing claims below refer to spiritual and light work. Do not ingest these stones. Keep stones out of the reach of children and pets, as they can pose choking hazards.

Agate: This stone is said to have dozens of uses, but psychics treasure it for its ability to absorb unwanted energies. And because agate is available in so many colors, it can also serve as a suitable substitute for other crystals of the same color.

Alexandrite: Promotes mental clarity and agility, and helps you to feel more connected to your environment.

Amber: This stone is said to help balance and maintain a healthy digestive system, as well as enhance memory and aid in learning.

Amethyst: Promotes mental and psychic clarity, connecting intuition and logic. It aids in good mental health, assists in meditation, and promotes good dreams.

Ametrine: This stone is said to be an all-around feel-good stone that can dispel depression and withdrawal symptoms. It's also said to be a powerful psychic enhancement stone.

Aquamarine: Encourages open and honest communication and helps you to communicate clearly and effectively. This stone is also said to have calming qualities. A wonderful intuitive aid.

Aventurine: Encourages the heart to grow and change in understanding and self-love. It is said to alleviate depression.

Azurite: This stone is said to assist in intuitive work, meditation, and dream work.

Bloodstone: The "stone of balance" is said to balance the mind, body, and soul, and it also aids the mind and heart when making decisions. It boosts courage and assertiveness, and is said to possess the ability to promote balance when dealing with blood-related ailments.

Carnelian: The stone of artists. Assists in creativity and motivation, boosts energy, and removes creative blockages. It is said to diffuse fear and bolster courage.

CAT'S EYE: This is said to attract wealth and prosperity, but more importantly, it's believed to be a mirror in which one can see the beauty of one's own soul.

CHRYSOPRASE: A useful grounding stone for meditation, especially when practicing outdoors and connecting with the elements of nature.

CITRINE: This stone promotes creativity and supports self-esteem. Diffuses feelings of unease and foreboding.

CRYSTAL QUARTZ: The "power stone" and amplifier of energy, it helps to clear the mind, elevate the soul, and boost all forms of energy and spiritual work.

DIOPTASE: A boon to those who are passionate about their work, this crystal creates and fosters a connection between the heart and the activities you're engaged in.

EMERALD: This stone is connected to the heart, and is believed to ease turbulent emotions and quiet disturbing dreams.

FLUORITE: A good grounding stone that helps you maintain focus. Quiets the heart and settles the mind. Balances and unites all chakras (energy power points) of the body.

GARNET: This stone boosts courage and aids in assertiveness. A high-energy stone, it fuels passion and creativity.

HAWK'S EYE: This is said to aid and magnify the third eye for visions and intuitive work.

HEMATITE: The grounding stone of all grounding stones (grounding stones keep you rooted, centered, and focused). An energy magnet, this stone absorbs feelings of stress and unease, as well as settles chaotic energy.

JADE: This is the love stone, promoting compassion as well as the strength for "tough love." It is said to dispel fear and create a sense of safety and security.

KUNZITE: This is a soothing stone that eases tensions and emotions. It encourages unconditional love and gentleness, and magnifies productive and creative feminine qualities.

Lapis Lazuli: This stone opens the third eye and enhances intuition and all types of mental work. Settles the mind and nerves from anxiety, insomnia, and depression. It is said to assist those afflicted with mental or nervous issues. Also, it opens the throat chakra, allowing for better self-expression and creativity. A protecting stone.

Malachite: Calms and soothes the heart and soul, and aids in meditation and dream work. It's a helpful stone for the ambitious business person, as it is said to attract wealth through hard work.

Moonstone: This stone calms emotions and helps energy to flow smoothly. It enhances visions and intuitive work by increasing awareness.

Opal: Opens the third eye and clears the mind for divinatory work.

Peridot: Considered a stone akin to turquoise, it calms the mind and eases bodily stresses brought about by illness.

Red Jasper: This stone energizes the body and boosts confidence. It is said to help with issues of abandonment and rejection. Enhances sexuality.

Rose Quartz: Brings soothing love, peace, and serenity to the heart, and beauty to the eyes. It is said to help relieve stress, tension, and depression.

Rutilated Quartz: This stone, with its very unique pattern, is said to be highly effective for spiritual work (like crystal quartz). It promotes balance and also assists in grounding.

Sapphire: This crystal assists with visions, helps with lucid dreaming, and aids in divination work.

Sodalite: A harmonizing stone that balances and aligns the heart and mind. It is said to assist you in remaining objective and focused on the conversation at hand. It is the perfect stone for anyone for whom debate is a part of the job (those working in law, politics, etc.).

Sugilite: This stone is said to be excellent for psychic and meditative work (like amethyst).

SUNSTONE: An all-around feel-good stone, believed to harness the uplifting and purifying qualities of the sun.

TIGER'S EYE: Helps to keep you focused and centered by separating thoughts from feelings. It tamps down anxiety and obsessive tendencies.

TOURMALINE: Eases a troubled heart and soothes the mind and soul. It is said to be a harmonizing stone.

TURQUOISE: A healing stone that promotes balance between the mind, body, and spirit. It opens the mind to healing knowledge and the heart to healing wisdom, focuses the eyes on faith and hope, and boosts speech communication.

SELECTING YOUR STONES

Many New Age stores carry crystals and gemstones. While you can get these stones virtually anywhere, please be sure to purchase your stones from stores you feel comfortable in. If the store is warm and welcoming, chances are that the stones will possess that same energy. If you feel the store is negative or conflicts with your intuition, seek your stones elsewhere.

Stores will usually have baskets of stones sitting around, with slips of paper telling you what the stones' properties are. While this is convenient, it is good to have a shopping list when you go in so that you don't impulse buy. (Remember, we're not trying to break the bank here.) Most gemstones are affordable, although others can cost you the equivalent of a down payment on a car. My opinion: the price of a stone does not determine the stone's worth to *you*. What determines a stone's worth in your practice is the vibration it gives off when you hold it, how much you resonate with it, and how much you feel it adds to your spiritual practice.

When browsing, hold the stones in your hands and don't be afraid to ask, "Do you want to come home with me?" Or, if you feel that you already can connect with an angel, ask your angel, "Will this stone add to my sacred space?" Empaths or clairsentients may feel a subtle vibration, a pulsing, or even a sudden shift in the stone's temperature. If the sensation feels comforting, you've made a connection and that stone is for you.

WELCOMING YOUR STONES HOME

Regardless of the chummy rapport you may have with your new stone, you must *cleanse* it before using it for any spiritual purposes. After all, you're not the only who stood there in the store talking to stones and asking which one wanted to come home. You want your stone to resonate and harmonize with *you*. To achieve that, you must first cleanse it of all the energy debris it may be carrying. Given that it has passed through the hands of the workers at the quarry, the tumblers, the packers, the shippers, the store clerk, and the hundreds of customers who came before you, there is no telling what types of residual human energy may be present. Stones are like energy magnets.

There are many ways to clear unwanted energies from stones.

CLEANSING BY SUNLIGHT: Wash your stone for a few minutes beneath a spray of cold water. Dry thoroughly! Set on the windowsill in the sunlight. A general New Age rule for cleansing stones in this manner is: three days in the sun, avoiding overcast days. Again, this is a general rule that many New Agers follow. As with everything, follow your intuition. Working with the angels is about breaking out of the bonds of rites and rituals, so if your heart tells you to use three hours of sunlight instead of three days, fine. Stones that respond well to sun energy include agate, amber, bloodstone, carnelian, cat's eye, crystal quartz, fluorite, garnet, red jasper, sunstone, and tiger's eye.

CLEANSING BY MOONLIGHT: Wash your stone for a few minutes beneath a spray of cold water. Dry thoroughly! Set on the windowsill during a new moon (two nights before and the night of). Why do I mention the new moon? Again, this is a general New Age rule that has been handed down through the ages from Earth religions. However, if you howl at the full moon like I do—and like Cassiel does—then by all means, use the full moon. This is *your* sacred space, and you have to feel comfortable with everything that lies within it. Stones that respond well to lunar vibrations include agate, amethyst, ametrine, aquamarine, fluorite, kunzite, lapis lazuli, malachite, moonstone, opal, rose quartz, rutilated quartz, sapphire, sugilite, and turquoise.

CLEANSING BY SALT OR SAND: Wash your stone under cold water. Dry thoroughly! Place the stone in a small brown paper bag and set the bag in a non-metallic bowl that you will use solely for the cleaning of stones. Cover the wrapped stone at least halfway (preferably completely) in sea salt or sand. Let it sit over night. Stones that resonate well with Earth energy include agate, alexandrite, aventurine, dioptase, emerald, fluorite, hematite, jade, peridot, and tourmaline.

CLEANSING BY AIR: Wash your stone under cold water. Dry thoroughly! In a small, nonflammable, heavy-metal bowl, burn three or four leaves of dried white sage. (White sage is a natural air and spiritual cleanser that has been used by Native Americans for centuries; it can be purchased at any health food store.) Once you get the leaves burning, blow on them gently to extinguish the flames, leaving the embers and their heavy aromatic smoke. Hold your stone over this smoke for a minute or two. Set it aside and leave it undisturbed for a day. From my experience, all stones respond well to this cleansing method—also called smudging—and I often use white sage during my meditation to cleanse the air. Stones that resonate well with air vibrations include citrine, hawk's eye, and sodalite.

Once your stone is cleansed, hold it between your hands for a moment and meditate upon it. How does it feel? Cool, warm? Smooth, rough? Get to know your stone. While doing this, you should take a moment to charge your stone.

Charging a stone is a New Age term that means "programming." Just as you can program your cell phone to do certain things, you can charge your stones to resonate with your energies. In essence, you are infusing your stone with intent, which is to bring harmony and peace to the sacred space. Also, those of you more inclined toward clairsentience may want to infuse the stone with the intent of it being a teaching tool, helping you become more sensitive to energy vibrations and vibrational shifts. Just as angels have energy signatures, so do stones—and I believe stones are useful tools in honing your ability to detect angel manifestations.

Once, when I shared this information with a client, she said that "charging" sounded a lot like "consecrating." And she's absolutely right. By charging—or consecrating—a stone, you're dedicating it to a specific purpose. Perhaps you wish to dedicate the stone to Archangel Raphael (amethyst/intuitive boost) or the Virgin Mary (rose quartz/divine love). If you wish, you may even say a prayer over the stone. Either way, an intent to aid you in your work is now programmed into that stone, and it is ready for use.

Once your stones have been prepared, they are ready to enter your sacred space. Where to place your stones is up to you, but I generally place larger stones (larger than the palm of my hand) on the floor beneath the table/altar or next to the entrance of the sacred space. Stones can either be placed on your altar or kept hidden away, only brought out as you see fit.

Remember, we're not crystal gazing here. That's for fortune-telling, and that's not what we're here for. We're here to improve our awareness of the world around us, a world in which our angels are ready to be noticed. The use of gemstones and crystals can most assuredly help us in our cause.

Candles for Illumination

When I light a candle… I feel the Presence of God move through me. When I look at that lighted candle, I know He is with me… communing with [me] through the practice of [healing].

—ELLA KAY, REIKI MASTER AND MY SPIRITUAL MENTOR

The use of candles dates back to ancient Egypt. Throughout history, candle technology has continually developed and today, even with fossil fuels and electricity, it is estimated that over a billion pounds of wax is used each year in the manufacturing of candles in the United States alone.

That's a lot of candles.

Over my years of working with candles, I've come to use them as luminaries only, not as a way to scent the meditation area. Candles that give off heavy scents contain lab-created, synthetic fragrances—which I consider a big no-no for spiritual work. The practice you are engaging in should be rooted in all things natural; therefore, your tools and accessories should be natural, or as natural as possible.

Candles can indeed be scented with essential oils rather than synthetic fragrances; these have a much more subtle bouquet and not the overpowering, headache-inducing scent I've often experienced from candles sold at mall candle shops. But it can be difficult to find essential oil candles, because the oils have a short shelf life once exposed to the light and heat. If your candle is advertised as being scented with "fragrance," it is highly likely this is a synthetic additive, which I suggest you avoid.

If you can get candles from a professional aromatherapist, awesome. Otherwise, it's best to stick with unscented candles. More than likely, you are going to use essential oils and/or white sage and/or incense in your sacred space anyway, and too many scents in a room can be unpleasant. The purpose of the candle in your sacred space is a simple one—to illuminate.

Selecting candles

I encourage you to make sure the candles you use are safe and of the highest quality. While paraffin wax candles are inexpensive and can be purchased virtually anywhere, some health experts claim that the wax creates carcinogenic smoke and therefore should be avoided. You can do your own research into this, and in my studies I've found reputable sources on both sides of this argument. But for personal health reasons, I try to refrain from using paraffin (which is a byproduct of crude oil). Beeswax and soy seem to be the naturist's choices for candles with reduced smoke and health impact (again, such claims are widely disputed). However, one type of candle I highly discourage you from using is the gel candle. It is made of a synthetic gel that has been known to pose a greater-than-normal fire hazard.

When selecting your candles, make sure that the wicks are lead-free. It is a common practice here in the U.S. to produce candles with lead-free wicks; however, candles imported from other parts of the world may not adhere to this standard. Read the label and be an informed consumer.

As far as the shapes of candle are concerned, I do not recommend the use of taper candles since they can tip or easily be knocked over. My personal choice are pillar candles, altar candles (poured into glass containers), and tea lights.

I believe altar candles that have been poured directly into their pillar glass containers are perfect for illuminating a sacred space. They are low maintenance and relatively safe—well, as safe as a candle can be. Use caution all the same. There are two drawbacks to such candles, however: (1) soot sometimes collects on the inside of the glass after prolonged use, which can be unsightly; (2) most of these candles are made from paraffin wax. Use your own discretion.

Furthermore, here is a proven tip I received from a local professional candle maker about pillar candles: their first burn should last one hour for every inch they are in diameter. So, if you have a pillar that is two inches in diameter, its first burn should be two hours. This eliminates flooding the well with wax and extinguishing the wick on the next burn.

In comparison to pillar candles, tea lights are low maintenance, inexpensive, and have incredible burn times (some lasting up to ten hours). Drugstore tea lights more than likely will be paraffin, but usually a New Age, religious, or health food store will carry soy or beeswax tea lights.

When selecting your candle, also make sure it contains energy conducive to your angel work. Refrain from selecting candles with trappings like "Love Attraction" or "Money Attraction." Such products were manufactured with a certain intent—magic. We're not doing magic here. We're not even doing divination. We're connecting with our brothers and sisters in spirit—something that is as natural as calling our relatives on the phone. Therefore, avoid these types of candles. Whether you find your love mate or not is already predestined; fervently praying for him or her to arrive while holding a love-attraction candle is pretty darn futile, if you ask me.

There are other candles sold that are dedicated to saints, angels, or gods and goddesses. These are fine, so long as you clearly understand the spiritual energy attached to the candle. After all, how do you know whether the person who poured the candle was really thinking about Archangel Michael or a fight she'd just had with a fellow employee? I mean, do you really believe that a Native American spirit candle made in China is genuinely going to be infused with the Buffalo Maiden's energy? Use common sense when browsing such items.

To that end, how about avoiding all the confusion and keeping things simple? Plain white candles that you yourself consecrate with intent—an intent to shed light and therefore illuminate your life path—are the best candles you could ever have in your sacred space. (Refer back to the section on charging crystals and gemstones for ideas about blessing your own candles.)

PRECAUTIONS

- Extinguish all candles when leaving the room or going to sleep.

- Keep candles away from items that can catch fire (clothing, books, paper, curtains, Christmas trees, flammable decorations, etc.).

- Use candleholders that are sturdy, won't tip over easily, are made from a material that can't burn, and are large enough to collect dripping wax.

- Don't place lit candles in windows, where blinds and curtains can close over them.

- Place candleholders on a sturdy, uncluttered surface and do not use candles in places where they could be knocked over by children or pets.

- Keep candles and all open flames away from flammable liquids.

- Keep candlewicks trimmed to one-quarter inch and extinguish taper and pillar candles when they get to within two inches of the holder or decorative material. Votives and containers should be extinguished before the last half-inch of wax starts to melt.

- Avoid candles with combustible items embedded in them.

- Keep candles up high, out of reach of children.

- Never leave a child unattended in a room with a candle. A child should not sleep in a room with a lit candle.

- Don't allow children or teens to have candles in their bedrooms.

- Store your candles, matches, and lighters up high and out of children's sight and reach, preferably in a locked cabinet.

- Try to avoid carrying a lit candle. Don't use a lit candle when searching for items in a confined space.

COMPILED FROM "CANDLE SAFETY," NATIONAL FIRE PROTECTION ASSOCIATION

One last word of caution: discontinue use of candles that sputter or pop. Sputtering and popping candles are defective—they have water droplets trapped in the wax. Such noises can be distracting during a meditation session. Also, the sputtering could pose an increased fire hazard if not watched carefully.

Scenting the Space

Although the word "aromatherapy" has been adopted to describe anything from artificially scented shampoos to designer car fresheners, as a spiritual practitioner you should not take the use of scents lightly.

The sense of smell is powerful. It can evoke thoughts, memories, and emotions in a nanosecond. The corporate world is highly aware of just how powerful the sense of smell is, and that's why food eateries are placed near major entrances of malls—the scent of food is uplifting and encourages shoppers to spend, spend, spend! Shopping malls throughout the U.S. pump the scent of fresh-baked cookies through the ventilation system to lull shoppers into comfort zones so that they stop thinking about their sore feet and start thinking about the larger-than-life cookies they used to eat when they were kids. Grocery stores also quickly learned that cooking hot food items on the premises encourages shoppers to spend more. As soon as you walk in the door, you're either hit with the aroma of roasted chicken (Thanksgiving dinner/family/home) or fresh-baked bread (ahh, more comfort). So, it is with great certainty that I can say that when used properly in your sacred space, scents can set the tone, relax your mood, and vastly enhance your spiritual experience.

Using Essential Oils

Essential oils are highly concentrated plant extracts, usually rendered through the process of distillation or expression. They are used in a myriad of applications, from candle making to food additives.

When considering aromatherapy blends for your sacred space, please select only essential oil blends. Dollar store and cheap knock-offs are filled with lab-created chemicals that actually could be harmful to the body and irritate the senses. To spot essential oil "fakes," all you need do is look at the packaging. If the oil is packaged in a clear bottle, there's a high chance that there is little to no essential oil in the product. Essential oils are sensitive to light and break down easily; therefore, they are packaged in dark bottles. Still, a dark bottle does not signify authenticity. Do your homework. Read the label. If the label says "fragrance," it is not an essential oil! Research your oils and know where they come from and how they are manufactured.

Essential oils need to be "blended," or put into carrier oils (usually vegetable based), before use. Unless you are trained and/or certified in aromatherapy, do not attempt to blend your own oils. Seek out a knowledgeable aromatherapist who is familiar with essential oil blends and can help you select the best ones for your needs. Also, remember to use your oil blend sparingly. A little goes a long way.

To use your essential oil blend, dab it lightly on your wrists or the back of your hands. (Be careful not to rub oil blends into your eyes.) I have a colleague who blends a special meditation oil for me that I actually dab onto my third eye, right between the brows. It's a practice I've been doing for years now, as a part of crossing myself when I pray and meditate. I'm not Catholic—and never have been—but I've adopted crossing myself, since I feel it is a powerful gesture that reflects the bond I share with Jesus Christ. As you get used to being in your sacred space, you too may find similar practices that inspire and encourage you along your spiritual path.

CAUTIONS

- Some oils may have contraindications and should not be used during pregnancy and breastfeeding, or if you have high blood pressure, diabetes, allergies, or other ailments. **Please consult a professional aromatherapist and your physician before using essential oils.**

- Never place a pure (undiluted) essential oil directly onto the skin, as it can cause serious skin irritation and even burns.

- Do not use essential oils or blends internally. Always follow package instructions.

- If an oil causes respiratory discomfort, discontinue use immediately. Also discontinue use if the oil causes headaches, sinus irritations, etc.

INCENSE

For many of us, spiritual work without incense is like cookies without milk. You can enjoy the experience, but the second element makes it so much better!

You can bring incense into your space in a variety of ways, but the most popular types of incense are sticks and cones. Basically, incense begins as a wood pulp that contains a flammable agent (potassium nitrate). After that, a natural adhesive, water, and aromatic materials are added. As with essential oils, stay away from grocery store brands of incense, as the chances are high that they contain more manmade ingredients than natural ones.

If you're unsure as to what type of incense to purchase, ask the people who own the store. This is why I encourage you get your items from stores that specialize in spiritual work, whether a New Age store or a Catholic supply store. Regardless of religious belief, both types of stores are focused on the spirit and the well-being of humankind; the employees should know all there is to know about the products on their shelves.

If you purchase incense imported from Asia, you will most likely discover that the incense does not have a stick at the end like typical Western brands do. There's also a high chance that the incense will be too large to fit into a conventional holder. This dilemma is easy to fix. Simply find a nonflammable bowl wide enough to catch the ash of the incense. Fill the bowl with sand, river stones, or rice, deep enough to hold the incense upright. Voila! Instant incense burner, Asian style.

Beyond store-bought incense, there are many other options for scenting your sacred space. Resin and herb forms of incense can be purchased in any New Age, religious, or health food store. Frankincense and myrrh are resins that can be burned over small charcoal disks especially made for indoor use. My personal favorite, and the only type of incense I use in my spiritual work, is white sage. This herb can be purchased in dried leaf bundles, and all you need to do is to light one or two leaves and then extinguish them, letting the embers create an aromatic smoke. Such use of sage and other plants and wood (like sweetgrass, cedar, and pine) has long been practiced in Native American traditions to cleanse, bless, and consecrate. I never begin my spiritual work without it, and if I am in a location where smoke is prohibited—like in a classroom—I just use an essential oil and holy water blend that contains sage extract.

Please take the same precautions with incense as you do with essential oils and candles, keeping both health and safety in mind. Be sure to refer back to those sections for suggestions and warnings.

Music

Music can have just as much of an impact on the atmosphere of your sacred space as scents do. While useful for tuning out the outside world, music can also be a helpful tool for enhancing your spiritual experience and helping to bring you closer to your angels. Archangel Raphael, for example, resonates with sounds that hark back to the days of valiant medieval knights and tales of dragons, wizards, and fairy folk; sounds of the flute and soft vocal harmonies can spark the imagination and boost your receptivity to the Angel of Healing. New Age and ambient sounds reflecting spiritual and space travel are also associated with Raphael.

Archangel Michael, on the other hand, resonates more closely with music that represents the body in motion, such as rock, hip-hop, dance, and tribal. While I think it may be a bit difficult to meditate to Metallica or Run DMC, soft ambient sounds (electric guitar, piano, or tribal chants from around the world) can relax the body and quiet your thoughts while still infusing your sacred space with music that best reflects this sunny angel.

Keep in mind that the goal of using music in your space is to help you focus on your spiritual work and connect with your angels and guides, so choose sounds that bring you a sense of peace and unity with the Divine. Michael is not going to balk or refuse to visit if you play Mozart. Raphael is not going to run for cover if you play bluegrass. This is more about what the music means to you, and the feelings it evokes for you.

The hunt for the perfect sounds can be daunting, but I generally recommend that my clients and students select music that calms the mind, body, and soul while evoking images of beauty and the presence of angels and guides. I suggest you refrain from music with lyrics, because lyrics can stir up thoughts, memories, or emotions that may be counterproductive to the spiritual task at hand.

But enough about "things." Regardless of how beautiful, helpful, or fun the afore-mentioned things are, they are just that—stuff you can do without. What is truly important in your sacred space is that you can sit quietly and reflect upon your life without interruption. You might find yourself meditating, praying, reading the Bible, or even working in this workbook. It doesn't really matter what you do in this space, as long as you remain focused on your spiritual growth. Don't balance your checkbook there; don't work on your office's proposal. That's not what the space is for. Rather, it is cordoned off for the sole purpose of enabling you to connect with your inner self and your angels.

On that note, keep the space free of clutter. Stack your books and notes neatly away and keep the items on your altar dusted.

Working Within Your Sacred Space

I don't believe that your frame of mind is all that important when you enter your sacred space. If you are feeling emotions like anger, frustration, heartbreak, or vexa-tion, don't let them deter you from finding solace in the place you've created as a refuge. Bringing your torrent of emotions with you is fine. What's important is that your sacred space is infused with enough tranquil energy to settle those emotions and help you to connect with your angels and guides, so that you can discuss the situations that are bothering you the most.

Because you visit your sacred space when you are happy as well as when you're upset (at least I hope that's what you're doing), soothing vibrations linger there. The intent with which you constructed the space will balance out those moments when you feel you'd rather launch a crystal through the window than meditate with it. This is why I cannot emphasize enough the importance of connecting with your angels during times of peace, and visiting your sacred space when you are already calm and focused. Doing so will train your mind and body to automatically shift into a tranquil mode whenever you enter the space with burdened shoulders.

But no matter how you enter this space, calm or otherwise, I recommend that you vocalize your intent the moment you sit down. As you set out your crystals or light your candles, get into the habit of blessing your space and inviting God to connect with you. Before you start the process of connecting with the angels, you can recite the Lord's Prayer or a psalm, recite a Buddhist chant, or be creative and invent your own little prayer. Doing so consciously prepares you for spiritual work. Even if you're upset, your mind, body, and soul will recognize that you have just entered a physical place of tranquility, and that now is a time to focus on communing with the realm of spirit in search of insight, wisdom, and healing.

A Note on Prayer

Prayer is beautiful. It is one of the healthiest things you can do for yourself, I believe, because it unifies the mind, body, and soul. Your mind is engaged because you're focused on connecting with your Creator; your body is engaged as you press your palms together, kneel at your bedside, or sit in a lotus pose; and your soul is engaged as you open up the channels, not only to send messages of love to your Creator, but to receive messages. Prayer is by far the best thing we can ever do as humans, because it can simultaneously soothe our downtrodden spirits, renew our strength, and invigorate our minds.

The fact that we are creatures of fate (participants in God's Great Equation) does not mean there is no need to pray. If anything, that's even more reason to pray! When we understand that life is scripted, we're less likely to go before our Creator begging for what might not ever be. Instead, we can go before God in total surrender, knowing that what will be, will be. This brings into sharp focus the words Christians have been saying for centuries: *Our Father, who art in heaven, hallowed be thy name. Thy kingdom come, thy will be done, in earth as it is in heaven…*

I repeat: *Thy will be done.*

So many of us have said this prayer, yet how many of us have truly reflected on what we were saying? By our request we are here; by our Creator's will we are here. And it is to our Creator that we should go in prayer with the following phrase in mind (regardless of what we want or what we desire): *Thy will be done.* Regardless of how we feel our life should be, *Thy will be done.* No matter how much pain and torment we are in, *Thy will be done.* Surrender is often the hardest lesson to learn.

But this is how to go to God in prayer—with our arms, hearts, and minds open and receptive to his will. This is the deal clincher. This is what determines just how well you will fare in establishing contact with your angels and spirit guides. If you are not ready and willing to accept that life may not turn out how you want it—that what you wanted to accomplish and what God wanted you to accomplish are two different things—I promise, you will have a difficult time connecting with the angels.

I know how difficult it is to pray and not ask God for something. After all, Jesus said, "Ask and ye shall receive," right? Well, when Archangel Gabriel first told me about fate and Michael started talking about God's Great Equation, I said, "Now hold on, you two. What happened to what Jesus said?"

And Gabriel quietly responded, "If you are of the understanding that you already have what God has intended you to have, you won't feel pressed to ask for anything." He then went on to remind me that if our minds and hearts are aligned with God's purpose, everything we ask is going to manifest. Everything. The key here is to focus our prayers more on aligning ourselves with God's Plan and less on how we feel our lives should be.

Once you get past the shock of this and push aside your stubbornness, you'll eventually throw up your hands and say, "All right, God. You win." And then you'll see things in your life begin to shift. One thing I've realized in the last two decades, as I alternated between obstinacy and surrender to God's Plan for me, is that when God instructs you to do something completely contrary to your heart's desire, don't be so quick to shoot it down. I've realized that much of what the angels have instructed me to do over the years proved to be learning experiences which moved me toward my personal goals—goals that always seem to coincide with God's Plan in ways I couldn't fathom. What seemed like detours were actually direct routes, and the more I saw this pattern occurring, the more I was willing to listen.

Now when I pray—even if I'm overcome with sadness and frustration—I listen.

Listen.

Remember what Archangel Raphael said: "Everyone prays for answers, but few stick around long enough to hear them." Prayer isn't just you walking up to the Maker, stating your grievances, and then walking out the door. Go before God, talk to the angels. Get everything off your chest, as it were, and then sit quietly and wait. The answers will come.

After your prayer, you can work in this workbook and hone your intuitive skills. You can converse with the angels casually if you don't have any pressing issues, or you can simply meditate. What you focus on while sitting in your sacred space is up to you, but understand the reason why you're here—not to plot out how to get back at your ex-boyfriend or tell off your boss in the morning, but to seek real solutions and real healing to whatever you're going through. Remember, challenges and obstacles are put before us to teach us; utilize your sacred space to meditate on what these things mean for you spiritually, and what they could possibly mean in the grander scheme of things. When I'm upset, I always remind myself that everything has a purpose and that God is in control at all times. And when I've been guilty of saying, "if God would just cooperate, I'd be in much better shape," I have to pinch myself and surrender all over again.

Your sacred space should be the one place you can go where you aren't beleaguered with a sense of struggle, but know that no matter what, everything is taken care of.

You will make it through just fine.

Grounding

If at any time you're still feeling out of sorts, try *grounding* yourself. No, I don't mean punishing yourself by sitting in a corner for a time-out. In electrical engineering, "grounding" is a method used to divert excessive electrical currents into the earth, keeping the currents from overloading circuits and causing damage. In spiritual terms, "grounding" means the same thing—we're not dealing with excessive electricity, but with the energies that flow from our thoughts, our emotions, and the spiritual environment around us. Some would call this *psychic energy*.

In essence, to ground yourself means to settle your mind, body, and soul. This can prepare you for any form of spiritual work, preventing you from getting swept up by emotions (especially those of others), thrown off balance by sudden energy or vibrational shifts, or being susceptible to unwanted energy exchanges. When you're grounded, anything that your whole being detects as excessive is immediately diverted to the ground beneath your feet. It's pulled away from your body much in the same manner as a tree diverts a lightning strike into the earth.

I always ground myself before any spiritual activity, especially when others are present. (For empaths and clairsentients, this practice is a must. They not only sense the energies and vibrations around them, but can also absorb these energies—both the pleasant and not so pleasant.) I encourage all of my students to ground themselves, as well as clients who work closely with the public. One little five-minute exercise can make a world of difference between being swept up in a storm or being in the eye of the storm, where everything is calm.

In my travels, people have shared with me dozens of different grounding methods. In the exercise that follows, I describe a very common method of grounding. As with everything else I teach, this method is customizable. Experiment with it and ask your angels for guidance on which method may work best for you.

Now, I fully understand that the process detailed in this Grounding Exercise seems to go completely against everything I said earlier about getting away from rites and rituals. The process is indeed highly ritualistic, but it is not something that you will need to do forever. The point of the exercise is to help you focus and calm your mind, so you can work on connecting with your angels and guides. Once you become proficient at focusing, this exercise—and indeed everything I say about sacred space—can be amended. You may get to a point where you don't need to vocalize intent upon entering your space; just the act of sitting down at your altar will be enough to prepare your body and mind for spiritual work. And after practicing grounding for a while, you will find yourself feeling solid and secure without having to go through so many steps.

So, yes, this exercise is a bit ritualized, but the point is to grow and be able to move past this stage, to a point where everything (from prayer to meditation to grounding) is so natural that it is less about going through the motions and more about getting the most out of your spiritual experiences.

❧ GROUNDING EXERCISE
Establishing Your Spiritual Roots

The objective of this exercise is not only to help you hone the skill of grounding, but also to encourage you to journal your progress. The questions below are presented so that when you review this exercise in the future, you can better gauge what external influences may help or hinder the development of your skill. When answering the questions below, try to be as specific as possible, so that you may be better able to pinpoint your strengths and weaknesses.

Remember, grounding is one of the most essential skills you will want to master if you're planning to engage in any spiritual work. It will relax your body, help clear your mind so you can remain focused, and rejuvenate your spirit for any tasks you plan to tackle.

Because grounding can benefit you in such a diverse way—in both your spiritual and mundane lives—I encourage assiduous practice until the skill becomes second nature.

Today's Date _____

Before you begin this exercise, indicate below how you're feeling today. Check all that apply.

☐ Angry
☐ Anxious
☐ Assured
☐ Cheerful
☐ Connected
   (in the present)
☐ Depressed
☐ Detached
   (wandering thoughts)

☐ Eh, I'm all right,
   I guess
☐ Fearful
☐ Frustrated
☐ Happy
☐ Hesitant
☐ Lonely
☐ Motivated

☐ Peaceful
☐ Skeptical
☐ Tired/Weary
☐ Uncertain
☐ Warm and toasty
   inside
☐ Worry-worn

1. Are there any specific events, recent experiences, or underlying reasons why you feel the way you do? Please provide a brief description.

_____

_____

_____

2. Why are you engaging in this exercise today?

☐ To prepare for spiritual work (meditation, prayer, connecting with the angels, etc.).

☐ To prepare for interaction with other people (school, the workplace, family, etc.).

☐ To prepare for interaction with large groups of people (a convention, church, concert, etc.).

☐ Other (please specify).

_____

_____

GROUNDING: STEP BY STEP

For beginners, it may be wise to document how long this exercise takes each time. This is not a race, but noting the time will help you better understand how time influences the results of grounding. As mentioned earlier, the more proficient you become, the less time it will take to effectively complete the exercise. But until then, it would be prudent to give yourself ample time to practice without having to rush.

1. Stand with your feet apart. Don't lock your knees, but make sure your stance is firm and stable.

2. "Cleansing": Lean your head back and take a nice, deep breath, allowing your belly to fully expand. Hold it for a few seconds as your health will allow and then bend forward at the waist to exhale and shake out your arms. Perform this inhale and exhale set three times.

   I was taught to make the exhale very audible—a heavy sigh as if you just unloaded a ton of bricks off your shoulders. At first I felt silly doing this, especially in a classroom with other students, but the vocalization of the exhale adds a sense of completion to this first step that I call the "cleansing." It's as if you're unloading the day's burdensome emotions and thoughts onto the floor before you. Ahh, it's a good feeling to let go of that excess baggage.

3. "Invocation": After the third exhale, ask your angels, ascended masters, or spirit guides to replace the unwanted energy you just unloaded with their bright, purifying light. Clairvoyants may visualize this. Clairaudients may hear a gentle humming sound. Clairsentients may feel that radiant warmth filling their bodies. Linger in the moment and welcome this exchange for a few seconds before moving on to the next step.

4. "Grounding": When you feel you're ready, take another deep breath and imagine the energy of the sacred Earth flowing from the ground, up your legs, and into your hips. Hold your breath for a few seconds as your health will allow and then exhale, pushing that energy back down through your firmly planted feet and into the ground. Note, you do not need to bend at the waist for this.

On the next inhale, bring this energy up past your hips and into your belly button. Exhale, pushing that energy back into the ground. Inhale and pull the energy up into your diaphragm, then exhale and push it back into the ground. Repeat these steps, each time moving a bit higher on each inhale. Next would be the center of your chest, then your throat, then the center of your brow, and finally up to the top of your head.

5. "Connection/Shielding": Once you've reached the crown of your head and exhaled, inhale again, this time pulling energy from the Earth and from Heaven to meet in the center of your chest. Imagine this vibrant light flowing from your heart and then encircling your entire body, protecting and nurturing you. Thank your angels and guides for their help and proceed with your spiritual work.

VARIATION

A variation I've been taught along the years is to imagine a glass, light-filled column lowering from Heaven over you, sealing you inside during the shielding step. A Native American colleague informed me that she imagined a glittering web of light being lowered over her like a cloak to catch unwanted energies and keep them at bay. And another image was that of bright, white angel wings folding around your body.

No matter the imagery you select for this exercise, your intent is the most important thing. So, once you enter your sacred space to connect with the realm of spirit, don't forget to announce your intent by way of prayer, and to ground yourself. By the time you do these, you'll be infused with peace and ready to engage your angels and guides.

Grounding: Afterthoughts

After completing the steps above, how do you feel? Check all that apply.

- ☐ Angry
- ☐ Anxious
- ☐ Assured
- ☐ Cheerful
- ☐ Connected
  (in the present)
- ☐ Depressed
- ☐ Detached
  (wandering thoughts)

- ☐ Eh, I'm all right,
  I guess
- ☐ Fearful
- ☐ Frustrated
- ☐ Happy
- ☐ Hesitant
- ☐ Lonely
- ☐ Motivated

- ☐ Peaceful
- ☐ Skeptical
- ☐ Tired/Weary
- ☐ Uncertain
- ☐ Warm and toasty
  inside
- ☐ Worry-worn

1. When practicing step five, "Connection/Shielding," what visualization did you use?

   _____

   _____

2. Is this visualization different from the last time you practiced?   Yes   No

   If yes, note any differences you may have felt during and after the exercise (for example, one visualization seemed more natural to you than the other).

   _____

   _____

3. How long did it take you to complete this exercise today?

   _____

4. If this length is significantly longer or shorter than the last time you practiced, did you notice any differences in how you felt during or after the exercise?
Yes   No

If yes, please indicate whether the time was longer or shorter and how this affected the results of your practice.

_____

_____

5. Additional Notes:

_____

_____

_____

_____

_____

_____

_____

_____

Meditation in Your Sacred Space

Many of the meditation books and audios on the market today focus on visualizing. And many people are left wondering why these materials fail so spectacularly to help them meditate. Everyone is able to visualize, right? Wrong. Not everyone can.

It isn't because there's anything wrong with these people; it is because their minds are programmed differently. This is neither good nor bad. It simply means that in order for me to be an effective teacher, I have to know how to speak a programming language that this portion of the population will understand. I too once assumed that everyone meditates visually, but have since learned that there are two types of meditators. For the sake of simplicity, I call them the *visionaries* and the *pragmatists*.

Visionaries are those people who can close their eyes and imagine they are standing in a vast green field surrounded by trees and mountains. They can feel the grass between their toes and the wind on their face, and even catch a hint of lavender in the air. Visionaries can completely immerse themselves and their emotions in a meditation with little to no effort, and hold images for quite a long time. I've been doing this since I was a child—at the time it was "daydreaming"—and so it was very easy for me to take up meditation in my teen years. Those who can visualize easily are often creative and imaginative folk who more often than not have their head in the clouds. They're often thinking of some distant, far-away land of times long past or far in the future. It's difficult for them to be in the moment, and they have to actively remain mindful of being in the here and now.

Pragmatists may have difficulty visualizing, but they have absolutely no problem pretending. Rather than "imagining" they are standing on a sun-kissed beach with white sands and the foamy surf tickling their toes, pragmatists can "pretend" that they are. You may ask "What's the difference?" Well, if you speak a different programming language, it's as different as night and day. For pragmatists, images need to focus more on action than on vision. They rely less on emotion and more on the act of "doing."

Where I would tell a visionary to imagine herself standing in a garden, I would tell a pragmatist to pretend she is walking into a garden, and then pretend to stop and pick a flower. When it comes to journeying inward, visionaries can take an image, run with it, and paint it vividly in their minds. Pragmatists benefit from a much more directed, step-by-step instruction.

Those who prefer such a checklist when meditating are very practical, grounded people. Their minds are analytical and they appreciate instruction that doesn't leave too much room for questions.

One of the funniest experiences I had while teaching a meditation class occurred a few years ago, when two young ladies attended for the first time. If there was ever proof that opposites attract, they were it. Apparently the best of friends, they sat close together in class, but I could tell instantly which one was more of a visionary and which one was more of a pragmatist. Wanting to test my hunch, I led the class in a short visualization experiment to gauge where everyone was. It was a simple task: imagine you are walking down a path to a sunny beach.

I then asked the students to share what they had experienced. The visionaries were seeing everything from sexy male models like those in romance novels, to mystical beaches with purple waters and purple skies, to unicorns flying over castles that stood high on rocky cliffs.

My poor pragmatist, however, looked at me with frustration and said, "You didn't say what kind of path led to the beach, so I couldn't figure out if it should be sandy, rocky, grassy, or brick!"

Her friend let out a long sigh. "You're supposed to come up with that on your own."

"Oh, so I'm the only unimaginative one here?" There was a long, awkward silence among the students that I quickly had to mitigate.

"It's not that you're unimaginative," I began. "You just have a more systematic way of thinking. I bet if I gave you a few minutes to plan out your journey, you'd be just fine."

"Yeah," my student said quietly. "I can't just jump into something like this if I don't know where it's going."

Knowing that I had a pragmatist in the class, I shifted the guided meditation to a step-by-step instructional, leaving little room for guesswork on the students' part. Visionaries might find such an approach a bit stifling, but let's be honest, visionaries can have a rebellious spirit and are going to envision whatever makes them blissful, no matter what I say. So, since visionaries can go with the flow either way, it was of very little consequence that I leaned the meditation more toward the pragmatist. If

I had continued guiding the meditation with visionary language, I'd have lost the pragmatist, and then I would have failed as an instructor.

For the most part, it's fairly easy to figure out who is a visionary and who is a pragmatist. If you are one of the many people who have had problems visualizing in a meditation, try pretending instead. Focus on pretending you are doing something instead of trying to think of images alone, and you should do just fine as you begin your journey inward to meet the angels.

Over the years, I've found meditation to be one of the most effective methods with which to hone the natural gift of connecting with the angels. For those of you who may be new to meditating, I set forth a process below that has netted the best results for my students. But first, let me remind you of some of the observations I made at the beginning of this book, about surrendering to God's Great Equation and opening yourself to its possibilities. Keep the following points in mind as you begin your meditation:

- Understand that you are a part of God's Great Equation and you will always be exactly where you're supposed to be when you're supposed to be there.

- Nothing happens by accident, so don't sell yourself short by calling validations "coincidences."

- Remember that you are a child of God, worthy of his love and worthy of his angels' guidance.

- Spiritual growth doesn't always happen overnight. Time and nurturing are necessities, so be patient with the angels. They will connect with you when they are meant to.

- Show gratitude every chance you get. Be grateful for every blessing, no matter the size, as well as for every challenge. Even during the most difficult times, lift your eyes heavenward and say, "Thank you." It is during those times when you will experience your greatest spiritual growth.

- Let go of the desire for specific results—this is an act of surrender. Remember that what will be, will be, and that no matter where the angels lead you, you are there for a reason.

- Abstain from judgment. In terms of spirituality, situations presented to us cannot be deemed as "good" or "bad." These are subjective notions dependent upon how you feel. Instead, situations should be seen as causes that spiritually propel you forward. Challenges, obstacles, and adversaries serve a purpose, so look inward and to your guides to discern what that purpose is.

Meditation Overview

The following "Chakra (Room) Walkthrough" Exercise is a fun meditation that guides you through a medieval castle corridor in which there are eight rooms. Once you have visited each room, you will find yourself in what I call your *Meditative Reality* (MR). Your MR should be a location where you feel safe and comfortable. It can be a garden, a beach, the house you grew up in, or even a church. (I've had a student imagine she was on a space station.) Whatever environment you feel secure in, that's where you go. The point is, this is the place where you will meet your angels and spirit guides, so it is important that you select a place where you feel at ease.

If you're adventurous like I am, you can leave it up to your angels to choose your MR. Quite often I have no idea where my MR is going to be. I enter my meditation with an open mind, ready for a new spiritual experience each time.

This meditation is a simplified version of what is generally known as a *chakra walkthrough*. Such meditations are quite common, but because the majority of them focus on visionary language, they may be difficult for some people to follow. I've been to too many classes where the instructor has led a walkthrough like this: "Visualize your root chakra. Notice how it pulsates or swirls. How does it feel to you? What do you see in your chakra? What is it telling you?" Now, for visionaries who know about chakras, there is absolutely no problem with this instruction; they can visualize the very abstract in their mind's eye. The pragmatists, however, along with those visionaries who aren't familiar with what a chakra is, will struggle with these seemingly straightforward instructions. Therefore, after offering a description of all the different chakras (presented as "rooms"), I offer two versions of this exercise: one for the visionaries and one for the pragmatists.

So, what is a chakra? According to the Merriam-Webster dictionary, it is "any of several points of physical or spiritual energy in the human body according to yoga philosophy." There are many chakras, all over the body, but the focus is usually on the seven main ones, which travel along the spine from your coccyx up to the top of your head. Each chakra acts like a minicomputer, influencing, monitoring, and recording the functions of assigned body parts, emotions, and spiritual dispositions. As you'll see through meditation practice, a balanced chakra creates harmony between the mind, body, and soul, whereas an unbalanced chakra can wreak havoc.

So, to guide everyone effectively along a meditation walkthrough without getting caught up in New Age jargon, I've modified the meditation so that each chakra is represented by a room in a castle (or whatever building you decide to use). As you progress through the meditation, you should pay much attention to each room and take note of anything that seems out of place. Occurrences such as a cracked window, severe weather outside, or an untidy room not only indicate your mental and spiritual dispositions, but can also indicate imbalances occurring in your body. (For example, piles of clutter in the Green Room not only suggest the unwillingness to forgive, but could also be a warning of bronchitis or other lung ailments.)

As with connecting with the angels, the Chakra (Room) Walkthrough meditation requires a lot of journaling in order for you to understand what different symbols mean. So, make a practice of walking through regularly, even if you're not seeking to connect with your angels and guides every time.

Another reason I use castle (or building) imagery in this meditation is because it seamlessly merges with finding your Meditative Reality. Through years of working with clients and students, I have found that those who perform a chakra walkthrough find it much easier to connect with their Meditative Reality than those who simply try to jump straight into it.

As your meditation skills grow and you find yourself able to ease into a state of relaxation at a much quicker rate, you'll be able to skip the walkthrough section of the exercise and go directly to your MR with little effort. I'm not suggesting that you altogether discard the chakra walkthrough once you've achieved this, however. It's an invaluable tool for balancing the mind, body, and soul, and can be of great benefit for calming emotions and lowering stress levels.

Chakra (Room) Walkthrough

The list below describes the rooms you will visit during your Chakra (Room) Walkthrough, en route to your Meditative Reality. All the rooms must be visited in the order listed. All except the White Room have one door; the White Room has two doors, one that leads in from the corridor, and one that exits out into the Meditative Reality. All except the White Room have a single window through which you can observe the world outside your building; the White Room has none.

In each room you will find an attendant who is the "voice" of your chakra. He or she may or may not speak to you, but it is always best to note their demeanor, as well as any information they may have to share. Pay attention, as this is actually your body expressing its strengths and weaknesses to you.

BLACK ROOM (VOID/INITIATION): There is much debate regarding the black chakra, since very few sources acknowledge it as a component of the main chakra system. While some metaphysical circles consider black the foundation chakra, they view it as the eighth chakra instead of the first. In my Reiki training and experience, I have come to understand that the black chakra dwells within the soul's perimeter but outside of the physical body, and serves as the foundation upon which the chakra system is supported. It represents our deepest spiritual connection to the Earth. It is the matrix, the darkness in which all life begins and germinates. It is where we begin our journey and, hence, the first room of the walkthrough meditation. Tidy, this room symbolizes stillness, surrender, and the willingness to connect with the Creator. In disarray, this room symbolizes reluctance, fear of the unknown, and an inability to recognize or acknowledge one's own spiritual identity as a child of God.

RED ROOM (SURVIVAL/MEDITATION): This room represents the first chakra (root), which is located at the coccyx. It affects the skeletal and muscular structures, as well as the adrenal glands. Some sources say it also affects blood, while others attribute the circulation system to the heart chakra. Go with what your intuition tells you. Tidy, this room symbolizes confidence, security, self-preservation, and stability. In disarray, the room symbolizes irresponsibility, fickleness, victimization, chaos, and ineffectiveness.

ORANGE ROOM (CREATIVITY/IMAGINATION): This room represents the second chakra (sacral), which is located just below the naval. It affects the bladder and urethra, reproductive system, and sex organs. Tidy, this room symbolizes creativity, motivation, reproduction, and healthy sexual/emotional balance. In disarray, it symbolizes callousness, procrastination, lack of inspiration, boredom, and clinginess.

YELLOW ROOM (INTELLECT/CLAIRCOGNIZANCE): This room represents the third chakra (solar plexus), which is located between the naval and the diaphragm. It affects the digestive system, liver, kidneys, and the pancreas. Tidy, this room symbolizes competency, self-reliance, self-sufficiency, and willingness to compromise. In disarray, it symbolizes extreme competitiveness, greed, low self-esteem, grudge-holding, and addiction to power and control.

GREEN/PINK ROOM (LOVE/CLAIRSENTIENCE): This room represents the fourth chakra (heart), which is located in the center of the chest. It affects the shoulders, chest, heart, lungs, thymus gland, and lymph nodes. Depending on your current disposition, this room may be green or pink. A tidy green room symbolizes a connectedness with humanity and feeling compassion and love for the self and others. A tidy pink room symbolizes a connectedness with all sentient beings and the experience and projection of unconditional divine or universal love. A green room in disarray symbolizes despair, emotional suffocation, fear, betrayal, and the refusal to forgive others. A pink room in disarray symbolizes spiritual guilt, the feeling of unworthiness before God, and the inability to forgive oneself.

BLUE ROOM (COMMUNICATION/CLAIRAUDIENCE): This room represents the fifth chakra (throat). It affects the neck, throat, ears, nose, mouth, and thyroid gland. Tidy, this room symbolizes expression, truth, and diplomacy. In disarray, it symbolizes the inability to connect and communicate effectively with others.

VIOLET ROOM (INTUITION/CLAIRVOYANCE): This room represents the sixth chakra (third eye), which is located at the center of the brow. It affects the brain, eyes, and pituitary gland. Tidy, this room symbolizes visualization, dreams, and the ability to see beneath the surface. In disarray, it symbolizes the inability or refusal to see the obvious, pessimistic thinking, and a general lack of wisdom.

WHITE ROOM (SPIRIT/DREAMS): This room represents the seventh chakra (crown), which is located at the top of the head. It affects the brain, nervous system, skull, skin, and pineal gland. Tidy, this room symbolizes enlightenment and a oneness with divinity. In disarray, it symbolizes illusion, lack of connectivity with reality, depression, and confusion.

Pointers before you begin

- Dress comfortably, preferably in loose-fitting clothing.

- Eat something light. It is difficult to meditate on an empty, growling stomach. Eating heavily, however, may make you sleepy during meditation. I have found that a light snack of toast, nuts, fruit, or raw vegetables is usually best.

- Sit in a comfortable position that you can maintain without having to shift often. I don't recommend lying down, however, for it's all too easy to fall asleep during a session.

- Allow yourself ample time to truly enjoy your meditation session. Having to be somewhere else by a certain time pulls your focus to the clock and may decrease the beneficial influences of the meditation.

- Make sure that you are not going to be interrupted during your meditation. Turn off the telephone and the television. Tell your family or roommates that you don't want to be disturbed for thirty minutes to an hour, and make sure they understand that your request is imperative. There's nothing more jarring than being in a conversation with a spirit guide or angel and have it interrupted by, "Hon, where'd you put the remote?"

- Allow yourself to be open and receptive. If you should feel emotions overflowing, let them flow freely. Healthy emotional release is a form of spiritual cleansing and is necessary for life balance.

- If you are not experiencing relaxation during the meditation, be objective and ask yourself what may be hindering you. Are you thinking about things you need to do, or something that's already happened that day? Try to put these things out of your mind by focusing on soothing music, a pleasing picture, or writing in this workbook.

⚭ MEDITATION EXERCISE: THE VISIONARY'S APPROACH
Chakra (Room) Walkthrough

Today's Date _____

How are you feeling as you begin this exercise today? Check all that apply.

- ☐ Angry
- ☐ Anxious
- ☐ Assured
- ☐ Cheerful
- ☐ Connected
  (in the present)
- ☐ Depressed
- ☐ Detached
  (wandering thoughts)

- ☐ Eh, I'm all right,
  I guess
- ☐ Fearful
- ☐ Frustrated
- ☐ Happy
- ☐ Hesitant
- ☐ Lonely
- ☐ Motivated

- ☐ Peaceful
- ☐ Skeptical
- ☐ Tired/Weary
- ☐ Uncertain
- ☐ Warm and toasty
  inside
- ☐ Worry-worn

PREPARATION

1. Prepare your sacred space as you see fit. Burn your sage, light your candles, etc.

2. Have a pen and your workbook/paper ready, for any notes you may need to take during the session.

3. Ground yourself and vocalize your intent.
   Example: *My intent for this session is to walk through my [castle] and discover what my chakras/body are telling me.   OR*
   Example: *My intent for this session is to connect with my mentoring angel/ascended master and to practice my intuitive skill of hearing (or seeing, feeling, knowing) through meditation.*

Walkthrough—Visionary Language

1. Enter your [castle] and settle into your surroundings for a moment. This is home, so make yourself comfortable before beginning your journey. Outside, the weather is beautiful and the sun is shining through the front door, illuminating the corridor that you will soon investigate.

2. Once you're comfortable, proceed down the hall to the first door on your left. This is the Black Room, where you will begin your journey.

3. Enter the Black Room and greet your attendant. Ask the attendant how they're doing and note their response. If your attendant has anything to share with you, take a moment to remember it for future review.

4. Explore your room, paying attention to anything that may seem out of place. Is the window clean or dusty? Is it raining outside now, or is it still sunny?

5. If you see anything in the room that needs to be repaired, do your best. Repaint walls, spackle over any cracks, clean up clutter, dust, or fix a light fixture. If you encounter any trouble in setting your room back in order, ask your angel or guide for tips and assistance when you talk to them later, in your Meditative Reality.

6. After you've examined the room and done all you can to restore it (if necessary), bid farewell to your attendant and exit.

7. At this point, you have some leeway. Your rooms can either be across from each other, or the corridor can cut straight through each of these rooms. The choice is yours. If you decide on the crisscross formation, then the Red Room (on the right) would be directly across from the Black Room (on the left). The Orange Room (on the left) would be diagonal from the Red Room. Yellow (right), Green/Pink (left), Blue (right), Violet (left). Visit all of these rooms and repeat steps 3 through 6.

8. The White Room is at the back of the mansion, at the end of the corridor. Enter the White Room, examine it, and talk to its attendant. Now it is time to enter your Meditative Reality. Open the back door of the White Room and step through.

9. Explore your MR and note where you are. Are you on a beach? In a temple? There is nothing to fear here, so feel free to go wherever your heart desires. It is here that you will connect with your angels and spirit guides. As you venture about, who do you encounter? Talk to them. If they wish to take you somewhere, follow. Record your experience in the spaces provided at the end of the exercise.

10. When you and your guides are ready to bid farewell to each other, a door of white light will appear. This door will lead you back into the White Room.

11. Now, in reverse order, visit each room again, noting any changes or information your attendants may provide.

12. Upon leaving the Black Room, head toward the front door and exit your building.

WRAP-UP

Take three deep breaths and allow yourself to slowly acclimate to your physical surroundings again. It is quite normal to feel a bit dreamy or out of touch after this
meditation. Give yourself time to regroup before going on with the rest of your day,
and please **do not drive or operate any heavy machinery until you are fully alert.**

1. Write down your experience below, paying special attention to "problem areas"
   and what they could potentially mean for you spiritually, mentally, and health-
   wise.

   _____

   _____

   _____

   _____

   _____

   _____

2. Also, don't forget to write down anything your attendants or guides may have
   said, so that you can refer back to the information as needed.

   _____

   _____

   _____

   _____

   _____

Questions if You Reached Your Meditative Reality

1. Did you notice any **exterior** anomalies before or during the walkthrough? **Example:** *Buzzing in the ear, sparkles of light, sudden shifts in room temperature, the feeling of weightlessness.* Pay attention to these anomalies, as this is the angels' way of calibrating your physical body to pick up transmissions.

_____

_____

_____

_____

2. Did anything special catch your attention as you visited each room in your meditation? **Example:** *The windows in the Yellow Room seemed dusty. It was raining outside the window of the Green Room.*

☐ No. Everything seemed to go swimmingly.

☐ Yes! I did notice something. (Describe what you saw and what you think it means.)

_____

_____

_____

_____

_____

_____

3. To what Meditative Reality (MR) did your walkthrough lead during this session? **Example:** *A forest, a beach, a train station, a city street, nowhere.*

_____

_____

4. Did you notice a shift in your emotions from the time you first entered this session to the moment you entered your MR? (Explain in detail how the MR environment made you feel.)

_____

_____

_____

_____

_____

5. Did this MR have any significance to you?

☐ No, I've no clue where it came from.

☐ Yes! (Explain. Use additional paper if necessary and attach it for future reference.)

_____

_____

_____

_____

6. Describe your MR in more detail. What did you see? Hear? Feel? (Note that "feeling" doesn't refer to your emotions; rather, did you feel the wind? Was it warm on the beach? Stuffy in the train station?)

_____

_____

_____

_____

_____

7. Did you find your guide?

☐ Yes. (Continue to next question.)

☐ Nope, he/she was nowhere to be found. (But go ahead and journal the other aspects of your experience. Also, see Troubleshooting Guide at the end of this exercise.)

_____

_____

_____

_____

_____

_____

_____

_____

_____

_____

_____

8. What did your guide appear to be?

☐ An archangel. (Continue to next question.)

☐ An ascended master. (Continue to next question.)

☐ A spirit guide. **Example:** *A deceased relative or loved one.* (Continue to next question.)

☐ Unsure. (See Troubleshooting Guide at the end of this exercise.)

9. Who do you believe your guide to be? **Example:** *Archangel Chamuel, St. Francis, Shiva.*

_____

10. How do you know?

☐ He told me.

☐ I know him (a friend, relative, loved one, etc.).

☐ I recognized his icons.

☐ I recognized him from books/artwork.

☐ I recognized his energy signature (the vibrations the angel was giving off).

☐ My intuition tells me I'm correct.

11. Was there anything about this guide that is consistent with what you know, have read, or have heard of him before?

☐ Yes. My angel was wearing white and playing a harp as we spoke!

☐ No. I had a hungry-looking wolf snarling at me and telling me he was Archangel Cassiel. *Nice doggie!*

    a. How did this inconsistency make you feel? **Example:** *Baffled, curious, surprised.*

    _____

    b. Did you ask your guide why he chose this appearance? If not, why do *you* think he chose this avatar?

    _____

    _____

    _____

12. Were there any exchanges of information between you and your guide?

☐ No. We just stood there like two cowboys at high noon.

☐ Yes. (Log it below.)

_____

_____

_____

_____

_____

13. Did your guide take you anywhere?

☐ No.

☐ Yes. (Where? Describe the destination.)

_____

_____

_____

_____

_____

14. Did your guide give you anything?

☐ No, shucks.

☐ Yes! (What was the item? What did he instruct that you do with it? What does the item mean to you?)

_____

_____

_____

_____

_____

_____

15. Describe your overall experience with your guide and this meditation.

_____

_____

_____

_____

_____

_____

_____

_____

_____

_____

_____

_____

_____

_____

16. After you bid farewell, did you conduct a reverse walkthrough?

☐ Yes. (Continue to next question.)

☐ No. (Why? **Example:** *Ran short on time, knock on the door.*)

_____

_____

_____

17. Did you notice any anomalies or changes in your rooms?

☐ No, they looked the same.

☐ Yes. (Describe and explain what these manifestations mean to you.)

_____

_____

_____

_____

_____

_____

_____

_____

How do you feel after this reflection? Check all that apply.

- ☐ Angry
- ☐ Anxious
- ☐ Assured
- ☐ Cheerful
- ☐ Connected
  (in the present)
- ☐ Depressed
- ☐ Detached
  (wandering thoughts)

- ☐ Eh, I'm all right,
  I guess
- ☐ Fearful
- ☐ Frustrated
- ☐ Happy
- ☐ Hesitant
- ☐ Lonely
- ☐ Motivated

- ☐ Peaceful
- ☐ Skeptical
- ☐ Tired/Weary
- ☐ Uncertain
- ☐ Warm and toasty
  inside
- ☐ Worry-worn

What are your final thoughts on the entire experience? Why do you feel this way?

_____

_____

_____

_____

_____

_____

_____

_____

ॐ MEDITATION EXERCISE: THE PRAGMATIST'S APPROACH
Chakra (Room) Walkthrough

Today's Date _____

How are you feeling as you begin this exercise today? Check all that apply.

- ☐ Angry
- ☐ Anxious
- ☐ Assured
- ☐ Cheerful
- ☐ Connected
  (in the present)
- ☐ Depressed
- ☐ Detached
  (wandering thoughts)

- ☐ Eh, I'm all right,
  I guess
- ☐ Fearful
- ☐ Frustrated
- ☐ Happy
- ☐ Hesitant
- ☐ Lonely
- ☐ Motivated

- ☐ Peaceful
- ☐ Skeptical
- ☐ Tired/Weary
- ☐ Uncertain
- ☐ Warm and toasty
  inside
- ☐ Worry-worn

PREPARATION

Pragmatists who are practicing this for the first time should read the entire meditation first, and then write down an answer to the following:

What type of building (castle, temple, mansion, etc.) will you pretend to use for your meditation? You should provide as many details about your building as possible, so as not to get snagged on them once you begin the meditation. For example, describe the type of doors that each room has or the type of furniture, if any, that may be in each room. How are your rooms decorated? Are you going for a particular motif?

_____

_____

_____

_____

_____

_____

_____

What type of an attendant will you discover in each room? Is the attendant male or female? Human or something else? (In my meditation, each room is attended by a Tara, a Buddhist female deity who is said to guide humans to enlightenment.) How will your attendants dress? Have fun with this, but make sure that you've answered any questions that may trip you up along the way.

_____

_____

_____

_____

1. Prepare your sacred space as you see fit. Burn your sage, light your candles, etc.

2. Have a pen and your workbook/paper ready, for any notes you may need to take during the session.

3. Ground yourself and vocalize your intent.
   Example: *My intent for this session is to walk through my [castle] and discover what my chakras/body are telling me.   OR*
   Example: *My intent for this session is to connect with my mentoring angel/ascended master and to practice my intuitive skill of hearing (or seeing, feeling, knowing) through meditation.*

Walkthrough—Pragmatist Language

1. Pretend you are standing outside your [castle], and the weather is sunny and perfect. When you are ready, enter your abode and walk through the foyer into the corridor where your rooms await you.

2. Enter the Black Room, on your left, and pretend that your attendant is there waiting for you. Perhaps she is happy to see you! Or, she may look a little despondent. Talk to her as you would a good friend and ask her how she is doing. Ask her how things have been since you last saw her and pretend that she is giving you answers.

3. When the conversation ends, explore your room. Pretend you are examining the furniture, the décor. You want to make sure that this room is in tip-top shape and that your attendant is happy with where she dwells. If you find anything amiss, pretend to repair it! Straighten a painting on the wall, dust your chandelier, or sweep. If there is clutter lying about, bag it and set it outside the room in the corridor. You can set it outdoors on your way back.

4. If you encounter any trouble in setting your room back in order, ask your angel or guide for tips and assistance later, when you talk to them in your Meditative Reality.

5. Pretend you're waving good-bye to your attendant and exit the room.

6. Go across the hallway to another door and open it. This is the Red Room.

7. You want to do here exactly what you did just moments ago. Pretend you're having a conversation with the attendant and note how her personality is different from the one in the Black Room. None of the attendants are the same, and they will all have something different to express (if they have anything to express at all). Examine the room and make repairs if needed.

8. Exit the Red Room, but don't forget to tell the attendant good-bye.

9. Now it's time to go diagonally across the hall from the Red Room to the Orange Room to perform the same exercises. Once you are done with the Orange Room, the Yellow Room is directly across the hall from it. Notice the crisscrossing pattern here. As you make your way down the corridor, the Orange Room is on the left, the Yellow Room is on the right, the Green/Pink Room is on the left, the Blue Room is on the right, the Violet Room is on the left. Visit each room and repeat steps 2 through 5.

10. When you leave the Violet Room, pretend you are walking to the door at the very end of the hallway. This is the White Room. Enter, pretend to greet your attendant, and explore the room just like you have with all the others.

11. When you feel you are finished in the White Room, pretend there is a door at the back that will lead you outside again. Walk through that door and pretend that you are now in your Meditative Reality.

12. Pretend to look around, because you are curious to know what this place has in store for you. This is where you will meet your angels and guides, so seek them out! Pretend you are fully immersed in your environment. For instance, pretend you are blessing yourself if you're entering a church, or pretend you're looking through an array of vegetables on a cart at the side of a dusty country road.

13. If you encounter someone, pretend to talk to them, asking who they are and why they are in your Meditative Reality. Write down their answers in the section that follows. Don't be shy. Don't be afraid. If they ask you to follow them, follow! You are perfectly safe here.

14. When you feel you are done exploring your MR, it is time to return home. No matter how far you may have traveled, the door leading home is only a step away. After you have said your good-byes, use your index finger and pretend you are drawing a full-sized door in the air or on a wall. When the drawing is complete, pretend that the door materializes and becomes real. This is your gateway home! Open the door and you will re-enter the White Room.

15. Now, in reverse order, visit each room again, noting any changes or information the attendants may provide.

16. Exit the building through the front door, but don't forget to grab any trash you may have left in the hallway to take to the curb for pickup.

Wrap-Up

Take three deep breaths and allow yourself to slowly acclimate to your physical surroundings again. It is quite normal to feel a bit dreamy or out of touch after this meditation. Give yourself time to regroup before going on with the rest of your day, and please **do not drive or operate any heavy machinery until you are fully alert.**

1. Write down your experience, paying special attention to "problem areas" and what they could potentially mean for you spiritually, mentally, and health-wise.

_____

_____

_____

_____

_____

2. Also, don't forget to write down anything your attendants or guides may have said, so that you can refer back to the information as needed.

_____

_____

_____

QUESTIONS IF YOU REACHED YOUR MEDITATIVE REALITY

1. Did you notice any **exterior** anomalies before or during the walkthrough? **Example:** *Buzzing in the ear, sparkles of light, sudden shifts in room temperature, the feeling of weightlessness.* Pay attention to these anomalies, as this is the angels' way of calibrating your physical body to pick up transmissions.

_____

_____

_____

2. Did anything special catch your attention as you visited each room in your meditation? **Example:** *The windows in the Yellow Room seemed dusty. It was raining outside the window of the Green Room.*

☐ No. Everything seemed to go swimmingly.

☐ Yes! I did notice something. (Describe what you saw and what you think it means.)

_____

_____

_____

_____

_____

_____

3. To what Meditative Reality (MR) did your walkthrough lead during this session? **Example:** *A forest, a beach, a train station, a city street, nowhere.*

    _____

    _____

4. Did you notice a shift in your emotions from the time you first entered this session to the moment you entered your MR? (Explain in detail how the MR environment makes you feel.)

    _____

    _____

    _____

    _____

    _____

5. Did this MR have any significance to you?

    ☐ No, I've no clue where it came from.

    ☐ Yes! (Explain. Use additional paper if necessary and attach it for future reference.)

    _____

    _____

    _____

    _____

6. Describe your MR in more detail. What did you see? Hear? Feel? (Note that "feeling" doesn't refer to your emotions; rather, did you feel the wind? Was it warm on the beach? Stuffy in the train station?)

_____

_____

_____

_____

7. Did you find your guide?

☐ Yes. (Continue to next question.)

☐ Nope, he/she was nowhere to be found. (But go ahead and journal the other aspects of your experience. Also, see Troubleshooting Guide at the end of this exercise.)

_____

_____

_____

_____

_____

_____

8. What did your guide appear to be?

   □ An archangel. (Continue to next question.)

   □ An ascended master. (Continue to next question.)

   □ A spirit guide. **Example:** *A deceased relative or loved one.* (Continue to next question.)

   □ Unsure. (See Troubleshooting Guide at the end of this exercise.)

9. Who do you believe your guide to be? **Example:** *Archangel Chamuel, St. Francis, Shiva.*

   _____

10. How do you know?

    □ He told me.

    □ I know him (a friend, relative, loved one, etc.).

    □ I recognized his icons.

    □ I recognized him from books/artwork.

    □ I recognized his energy signature (the vibrations the angel was giving off).

    □ My intuition tells me I'm correct.

11. Was there anything about this guide that is consistent with what you know, have read, or have heard of him before?

    □ Yes. My angel was wearing white and playing a harp as we spoke!

    □ No. I had a hungry-looking wolf snarling at me and telling me he was Archangel Cassiel. *Nice doggie!*

a. How did this inconsistency make you feel? **Example:** *Baffled, curious, surprised.*

_____

b. Did you ask your guide why he chose this appearance? If not, why do *you* think he chose this avatar?

_____

_____

_____

12. Were there any exchanges of information between you and your guide?

☐ No. We just stood there like two cowboys at high noon.

☐ Yes. (Log it below.)

_____

_____

_____

_____

_____

_____

_____

13. Did your guide take you anywhere?

☐ No.

☐ Yes. (Where? Describe the destination.)

_____

_____

_____

_____

_____

14. Did your guide give you anything?

☐ No, shucks.

☐ Yes! (What was the item? What did he instruct that you do with it? What does the item mean to you?)

_____

_____

_____

_____

_____

15. Describe your overall experience with your guide and this meditation.

_____

_____

_____

_____

_____

_____

_____

_____

_____

_____

_____

_____

_____

_____

16. After you bid farewell, did you conduct a reverse walkthrough?

☐ Yes. (Continue to next question.)

☐ No. (Why? **Example:** *Ran short on time, knock on the door.*)

_____

_____

_____

17. Did you notice any anomalies or changes in your rooms?

☐ No, they looked the same.

☐ Yes. (Describe and explain what these manifestations mean to you.)

_____

_____

_____

_____

_____

_____

_____

_____

How do you feel after this reflection? Check all that apply.

- ☐ Angry
- ☐ Anxious
- ☐ Assured
- ☐ Cheerful
- ☐ Connected
  (in the present)
- ☐ Depressed
- ☐ Detached
  (wandering thoughts)

- ☐ Eh, I'm all right,
  I guess
- ☐ Fearful
- ☐ Frustrated
- ☐ Happy
- ☐ Hesitant
- ☐ Lonely
- ☐ Motivated

- ☐ Peaceful
- ☐ Skeptical
- ☐ Tired/Weary
- ☐ Uncertain
- ☐ Warm and toasty
  inside
- ☐ Worry-worn

What are your final thoughts on the entire experience? Why do you feel this way?

_____

_____

_____

_____

_____

_____

_____

_____

_____

_____

Meditation Troubleshooting Guide

I'm having difficulty getting through either approach to the meditation.

Don't worry. There are several other methods you can try that may increase your success rate. All of these variations are based on the Pragmatist's Approach, which is better suited to those encountering problems with meditation.

(1) My first suggestion is to practice with a friend. After preparing for the meditation as usual, have your friend dictate the steps of the walkthrough to you. This way, you will be prompted about each step without having to break your concentration to check on them. If you find it distracting to have another person present, a variation on this approach is to record the walkthrough instructions yourself, then play them back when you meditate.

(2) Another method is to write a walkthrough "script," in which you change the walkthrough instructions into a first-person narrative of your progress through the rooms. For example: *I am now walking into the Black Room. I am greeting my attendant. I am now inspecting the Black Room a moment to make sure everything is in order.* As in method #1, you can either have a friend read the script to you or record it and play it back later. Using the script method will greatly reduce any distractions that may be inhibiting your ability to focus.

(3) If you find that just listening to your script still doesn't help, try repeating aloud each line in the script as you meditate. When you hear *I am now walking into the Black Room*, you repeat, "I am now walking into the Black Room," etc.

Keep in mind that the simple act of writing out your script, in a quiet environment with no distractions, is a meditation in its own right. Not only does it help you organize your thoughts, but it helps to clear your mind as well—because you're unloading, onto the paper, any mental chatter that has been hindering your concentration.

Whether writing down your meditation, vocalizing it, or simply listening to it, be sure to assess how the rooms appear each time you meditate. For example: *The Black Room is clean, and I am safe here. I can now visit the Red Room.* Each time you meditate, what you feel or what your intuition tells you about the rooms may be different. On Monday, the Black Room may be in order. But on Friday, the Black Room may be in disarray.

Also, if you go all the way to your Meditative Reality, you can choose write about it much like you would write a story. It may seem like what you're writing is coming from your imagination, but as I've said several times before, your imagination is a bridge to your intuition. The imagination can guide us past the filters of the mind and straight into the spiritual experience of an angelic encounter, so don't discount it!

My angel (guide) didn't meet me in my Meditative Reality.

If this happens, just explore your MR and connect with the environment through the methods you wish to engage: clairvoyance, clairaudience, clairsentience. For those of you practicing claircognizance, are there any books in your MR? Browse through them!

If you still do not connect with a guide, linger in your MR as long as you wish, log your experience, and do a reverse walkthrough. Don't be disappointed that you didn't connect with anyone. The angels simply saw fit to not distract you from whatever you were gleaning from your MR. Thank them just the same, and have confidence that they'll connect with you when you're ready.

My angel (guide) appeared, but I'm unsure who it is.

If the presence of this being does not cause you any anxiety or foreboding, by all means engage it and see who it is! If, however, it makes you uneasy, ask it to go away. If it refuses, don't panic. It can't harm you. Instead, ask yourself what this being's appearance could mean. After all, nothing happens in this world without God's permission; hence, this entity has a purpose. This situation requires some objective soul-searching, so return to the White Room, regroup, and end the session with a prayer for understanding.

Don't let yourself be daunted by this kind of experience. I was haunted for a decade by an entity I encountered in a dreamscape, until I finally realized it was just a manifestation of the fears and doubts I was feeling about my spirituality and relationship with God. Such demons can and will manifest along your spiritual journey, but they are not below our feet, roasting souls in pits of fire. They dwell inside, taking the form of fear, guilt, anger, victimization, and envy, just to name a few.

Like Hollywoodized demons, these evil entities can be fierce, unrelenting, and destructive foes, but they have a weakness. Everything has an *off* switch, and it'll

be your job to figure out what that is—be it asking someone for forgiveness, forgiving yourself, letting go of grudges, or facing your worst nightmares. You can't
fight these demons; that's like trying to fight the darkness. You can't kung fu or box
against darkness, but you can bring light to it. It's the only way to dispel it. Therefore, bring light to that which haunts you the most by being honest with yourself
and continually relying on the fact that no matter what, you are a beloved child of
God. Do this, and those demons will cease to impede your spiritual work. This is
all part of spiritual growth—there is no way around it. At one point or another in
our lives, we must face and conquer these manifestations.

Want a clue as to what the entity you have met might reflect? Do another walkthrough meditation and explore each room carefully. Look for dirty, cracked windows, cobwebs, clutter, foul smells, or adverse weather outside. Also, if you have
attendants in each room, note their demeanor. That can be a huge clue as to what
you need to reexamine in your life, and will set in motion the actions needed to
promote healing and balance.

5

ANGELIC
MANIFESTATIONS

WELL, MY FRIEND, I HOPE that by now you've discovered, through the glimpses I've shown you, how beautiful, how wondrous, and how majestic our archangel companions are. Helpful and compassionate, loving and wise, they dutifully walk beside us as our brothers and sisters in spirit, offering their guidance and careful nurturing.

So, no matter how you approach the angels, whether through clairaudience, clairsentience, or any of the myriad of intuitive gifts, know in your heart that your angels will never judge you or abandon you. They are steadfast and loyal to your spiritual cause—that is, to the divinely ordained purpose for which you exist in this reality at this particular time. I encourage you to reach out and invite them into your personal world, so that you may be able to truly enjoy their presence and reap the greatest benefit possible from all they have to teach you in this lifetime. I encourage you to open the channels to their beautiful radiance and their limitless love and allow them to inspire, hearten, and comfort you as you continue to walk this spiritual journey. Of course, they're going to remain by your side regardless of your awareness of them, but imagine just how much richer each experience you have can be when you are open and receptive to their divine splendor.

You've no doubt tinkered with several of the exercises in this book before getting to this point, but long before the angels guided you to *The Angel Code*, you may very well have already been connecting with them. You just weren't aware of it yet! I've had countless clients come to me after reading *Azrael Loves Chocolate* and say that they had been connecting with their angel guides all their lives, but hadn't realized it until they gained an understanding of how the angels work and manifest in our reality.

So, to help you see the angels in action, I've provided the following Life Log. It's a very general log designed to help you keep track of your connections and communications with your angels, ascended masters, and spirit guides. You can use it however you choose in your daily life, whether to record casual conversations with the angels or to call upon the angels for help working through specific situations. This log can also serve as a dream or meditation journal, if you choose. As always, you may want to photocopy the blank pages and keep them in a binder.

Remember, while you can always call on specific archangels that you'd like to connect with, each angel has a relevant time and place in your life. The focus of your log should be on building up your ability to connect *in general*. And as you write down your angel's insights, along with any validation signs you receive, you will have documentation of the amazing growth of your intuitive skills.

And you will get to watch the angels' messages manifesting in your life!

The more you engage with your angels, and the more you exchange with them, the better you will get to know…yourself. As you jump the hurdles of everyday life, journaling your connections will help you become less skeptical and/or bolster your belief. When validation signs manifest, journal the experience and allow it to serve as a building block of your faith. Faith not just in your angels, but in your own intuitive gifts—and in yourself as a child of God.

⟨ᴿ LIFE LOG
Angel Encounters

Today's Date _____

How are you feeling today? Check all that apply.

- ☐ Angry
- ☐ Anxious
- ☐ Assured
- ☐ Cheerful
- ☐ Connected
  (in the present)
- ☐ Depressed
- ☐ Detached
  (wandering thoughts)

- ☐ Eh, I'm all right,
  I guess
- ☐ Fearful
- ☐ Frustrated
- ☐ Happy
- ☐ Hesitant
- ☐ Lonely
- ☐ Motivated

- ☐ Peaceful
- ☐ Skeptical
- ☐ Tired/Weary
- ☐ Uncertain
- ☐ Warm and toasty
  inside
- ☐ Worry-worn

Describe your emotional state: _____

_____

_____

CIRCUMSTANCES

Why are you choosing to connect with the angels today?: _____

_____

_____

_____

_____

If there is a specific situation motivating you, what are your feelings toward this situation? _____

_____

_____

_____

If dealing with a specific situation, are you held to any particular deadlines?

_____

NATURE OF CONNECTION

☐ Attempt made to connect with _____ (Archangel's Name).

☐ Two-way connection established with _____ (Archangel's Name).

METHOD OF CONNECTION

☐ Clairaudience ☐ Claircognizance ☐ Signs
☐ Clairvoyance ☐ Intuition ☐ Meditation
☐ Clairsentience ☐ Dreams
☐ Other (cards, pendulum, etc.)

If "Other," specify which method: _____

_____

_____

DESIRED RESULTS

What do you hope will happen as a result of this connection? (Hold hope in your heart, but remember, we all must surrender to God's will.)

_____

_____

_____

If your desired result comes to pass (cause), what do you believe will arise from it (effect)?

_____

_____

If your desired result does not come to pass (cause), what do you believe will arise from it (effect)?

_____

_____

YOUR ANGEL'S GUIDANCE

Write down the guidance or insights your angel offered. Be as specific as possible, and include any dates or numbers that seem significant.

_____

_____

_____

_____

_____

_____

VALIDATION REQUEST

Ask your angel to validate this communication by sending some sort of sign. What sign does your angel say to watch for?

_____

_____

How are you feeling now? Check all that apply, and explain.

- ☐ Angry
- ☐ Anxious
- ☐ Assured
- ☐ Cheerful
- ☐ Connected
  (in the present)
- ☐ Depressed
- ☐ Detached
  (wandering thoughts)

- ☐ Eh, I'm all right,
  I guess
- ☐ Fearful
- ☐ Frustrated
- ☐ Happy
- ☐ Hesitant
- ☐ Lonely
- ☐ Motivated

- ☐ Peaceful
- ☐ Skeptical
- ☐ Tired/Weary
- ☐ Uncertain
- ☐ Warm and toasty
  inside
- ☐ Worry-worn

_____

_____

_____

Progress and Validation Updates

Record your progress (in life, or in a specific situation) as it relates to the initial angel connection documented above. Do this regularly, and especially when signs manifest that validate the communication.

Today's Date _____

Did you receive a sign? What was it? _____

_____

Progress _____

_____

Today's Date _____

Did you receive a sign? What was it?_____

_____

Progress _____

_____

Today's Date _____

Did you receive a sign? What was it?_____

_____

Progress _____

_____

Today's Date _____

Did you receive a sign? What was it?_____

_____

Progress _____

_____

Today's Date _____

Did you receive a sign? What was it?_____

_____

Progress _____

_____

FINAL REFLECTIONS, OR RESOLUTION OF SITUATION

_____

_____

_____

_____

_____

_____

BIBLIOGRAPHY

Andrews, Ted. *Animal Speak.* St. Paul, MN: Llewellyn, 2008.

Biggs, Matthew, Jekka McVicar, and Bob Flowerdew. *Vegetables, Herbs and Fruit: An Illustrated Encyclopedia.* New York: Firefly Books, 2008.

Braden, Gregg. *The Divine Matrix.* Carlsbad, CA: Hay House, 2006.

Bunson, Matthew. *Angels A to Z: A Who's Who of the Heavenly Host.* New York: Three Rivers Press, 1996.

Consumer Product Safety Commission. "CPSC, Nature's Finest Announce Recall of Gel Candles." http://www.cpsc.gov/cpscpub/prerel/prhtml05/05143.html. (accessed April 2009).

Coombes, Allen J. *Smithsonian Handbooks: Trees.* New York: Dorling Kindersley, 2002.

Cunningham, Scott. *The Complete Book of Incense, Oils and Brews.* St. Paul, MN: Llewellyn, 2008.

———. *Cunningham's Encyclopedia of Magical Herbs.* St. Paul, MN: Llewellyn, 2008.

Davidson, Gustav. *A Dictionary of Angels: Including the Fallen Angels.* New York: The Free Press, 1967.

Davis, Patricia. *Aromatherapy: An A-Z: The Most Comprehensive Guide to Aromatherapy Ever Published.* London: Random House, 2005.

Eason, Cassandra. *The Illustrated Directory of Healing Crystals.* London: Collins & Brown, 2003.

Embree, Ainslee. *Sources of Indian Tradition.* New York: Columbia University Press, 1988.

Guiley, Rosemary. *The Encyclopedia of Saints.* New York: Checkmark Books, 2001.

Hypnosis Motivation Institute. *Foundations in Hypnotherapy.* Tarzana, CA: Panorama Publishing, 2006.

Holy Bible. Authorized King James Version. Nashville: Thomas Nelson, 2003.

Kaplan, Aryeh. *Sefer Yetzirah: The Book of Creation.* York Beach, ME: Red Wheel/ Weiser, 1997.

Keel, Othmar. *Gods, Goddesses, and Images of God.* London: T&T Clark Publishers, 2001.

Klinger-Omenka, Ursula. *Reiki with Gemstones.* Twin Lakes, WI: Lotus Light Publications, 1997.

Lake-Thom, Bobby. *Spirits of the Earth: A Guide to Native American Nature Symbols, Stories and Ceremonies.* New York: The Penguin Group, 1997.

Lewis, James R., and Dorothy Oliver. *Angels A to Z.* Canton, MI: Visible Ink Press, 2002.

Lindow, John. *Norse Mythology: A Guide to Gods, Heroes, Rituals, and Beliefs.* New York: Oxford University Press, 2001.

Martin, Richard P. *Myths of the Ancient Greeks.* New York: The Penguin Group, 2003.

Myss, Caroline, Ph.D. *Anatomy of the Spirit.* New York: Three Rivers Press, 1996.

Naiman, Rubin R., PhD. *Healing Night: The Science and Spirit of Sleeping, Dreaming and Awakening.* Minneapolis: Syren Book Company, 2006.

National Candle Association. "Facts and Figures." http://www.candles.org/about_facts.html (accessed April 2009).

National Fire Protection Association. "Candle Safety." http://web.archive.org/web/20020209193415/%20http://www.nfpa.org/Research/nfpafactsheets/candlesafety/candlesafety.asp (accessed April 2009).

Rock, Andrea. *The New Science of How and Why We Dream*. New York: Basic Books, 2004.

Silverman, David P. *Ancient Egypt*. New York: Oxford University Press, 1997.

Simpson, Liz. *The Book of Chakra Healing*. New York: Sterling Publishing, 1999.

Taylor, Terry Lynn. *Messengers of Light: The Angels' Guide to Spiritual Growth*. Tiburon, CA: H.J. Kramer, 1990.

Turner, Patricia, and Charles Russell Coulter. *Dictionary of Ancient Deities*. New York: Oxford University Press, 2000.

Too, Lilian. *The Complete Illustrated Guide to Feng Shui*. New York: HarperCollins, 2001.

Virtue, Doreen. *Archangels & Ascended Masters*. Carlsbad, CA: Hay House, 2003.

Other Resources

Mountain Rose Herbs, http://www.mountainroseherbs.com

Nurtured by Mother Nature, http://www.nurturedbymothernature.com

INDEX

To Write to the Author

If you wish to contact the author or would like more information about this book, please write to the author in care of Llewellyn Worldwide and we will forward your request. Both the author and publisher appreciate hearing from you and learning of your enjoyment of this book and how it has helped you. Llewellyn Worldwide cannot guarantee that every letter written to the author can be answered, but all will be forwarded. Please write to:

Chantel Lysette
c/o Llewellyn Worldwide
2143 Wooddale Drive
Woodbury, MN 55125-2989

Please enclose a self-addressed stamped envelope for reply,
or $1.00 to cover costs. If outside the U.S.A., enclose
an international postal reply coupon.

Many of Llewellyn's authors have websites with additional information and resources. For more information, please visit our website at:

www.llewellyn.com